Charles Sangster

By W. D. HAMILTON

Twayne Publishers, Inc.   ::   New York

88405

To Dr. Desmond Pacey

*In gratitude for his
inspiring teaching*

Go once again, my old-time bark,
  And brave the perils of the sea,
'Neath clear blue skies, o'er north seas dark,
  And send glad tidings back to me.

The weary decades hast thou lain
  At anchor in the land-locked bay;
Go, seek some mart across the main,
  Or stand or founder by the way.

Though many a craft of broader sweep,
  Fresh from some Paradise of Smiles,
Dips like a plummet through the deep,
  Or parts upon the coral isles:

Though many a sail with fair device,
  By perfumed summer breezes blown,
Past flowery shores, through isles of spice,
  Has passed into the dim unknown:

For hope is sweet as maiden love,
  And sweet as maiden fancies are;
His sun is ever bright above,
  And never sets his polar star.

Then once again, my old-time bark,
  Go, brave the perils of the sea,
Though thou should'st wander down the dark,
  And send no message back to me.

              —Charles Sangster
              (from an unpublished fragment)

Preface

"It would be quite fatuous," observed Desmond Pacey in his *Ten Canadian Poets*, "to bring to bear upon Sangster's poetry the heavy guns of either the new or the old criticism." In *Charles Sangster* I have tried to maintain a critical posture, but I have also attempted to present as much factual information as possible about Sangster's life and poetry. Half-page biographical sketches and sweeping evaluative statements are not difficult to find, but little biographical detail has been published, and the majority of the poems have not been commented upon by either critic or historian. I have therefore regarded biographical data as important, and I have endeavored to mention, at least, most of the poems.

The pattern of Sangster's life and work dictated the book's structure. Chapter 1 is a chronologically ordered biographical account of Sangster's life prior to the publication of his first volume, and Chapters 2 and 3 deal descriptively with his literary career. Chapters 4, 5, and 6 are critical surveys of *The St. Lawrence and the Saguenay*, *Hesperus*, and the unpublished work, respectively. In these chapters Sangster's work is liberally quoted, and in Chapter 6 a number of the unpublished poems are presented whole. One reason for this is that the characteristics of verse such as Sangster wrote are often quite readily apparent, making illustration preferable at times to explanation. A more important reason though is that the reader would not otherwise have access to Sangster's lines, because the poetry, indeed if it was ever published, has been out of print for over a hundred years. Chapter 7 is both summary and assessment. In it consideration is given to Sangster's basic ideas, his "Canadianism," the influences which shaped his work, and his poetic achievement relative to that of his Canadian predecessors, contemporaries, and successors.

W. D. HAMILTON

Fredericton, New Brunswick

Acknowledgments

For permission to quote from the following works, I am indebted to these writers and publishers: Desmond Pacey, *Ten Canadian Poets*, Ryerson Press; A. J. M. Smith, *The Book of Canadian Poetry*, W. J. Gage Limited; and H. Pearson Gundy, "Charles Sangster 1822–1893," *Historic Kingston* (Kingston Historical Society).

I am very thankful to Dr. Desmond Pacey for first arousing my interest in Canadian literary history, for guiding my early inquiries into Charles Sangster's work, and for continuing to encourage and assist me at every opportunity. I have also to thank Professor H. Pearson Gundy of Queen's University for his personal interest and assistance; the staffs of the Reference Division and Archives of the Douglas Library at Queen's for their cooperation; my sister Elinor Leach of Ottawa for searching census and other records for me at the Public Archives; my wife, Vy, for her patient understanding; and finally my editor, Professor Joseph Jones of the University of Texas at Austin, for the intelligence and courtesy of his criticisms.

Contents

Chronology

1822 Charles Sangster born (July 16) at the Navy Yard, Point Frederick, Kingston, Upper Canada, son of James and Ann Ross Sangster. Twin sister dies in infancy.

1824 James Sangster, the poet's father, dies.

1830's Attends school for a few years in Kingston.

1837 Obtains his first job—with the Ordnance Department at Fort Henry, Kingston, where he remains until 1849, working part time also in the newspaper office of the *British Whig*, Kingston.

1849 Becomes editor of the Amherstburg *Courier*, Amherstburg, Canada West, for a few months, returning soon to Kingston as subeditor of the *British Whig*.

1850 Publishes poems in the *Literary Garland*. This marks the beginning of a lengthy period of publication in leading Canadian journals.

1856 Publishes *The St. Lawrence and the Saguenay and Other Poems*. Marries Mary Kilborn, of Kingston.

1858 Mary Kilborn Sangster dies of pneumonia at the age of twenty-two.

1860 Publishes *Hesperus and Other Poems and Lyrics*. Marries Henrietta Charlotte Mary Meagher, of Kingston.

1868 Accepts appointment to a clerical position with the Post Office Department, Ottawa.

1870's Ill health and overwork hamper literary activity.

1886 Retires from the Post Office Department in broken health, and returns to live in Kingston.

1886– Attempts to put in order for publication revisions of his
1893 published volumes as well as two unpublished volumes: "Norland Echoes and Other Strains and Lyrics," and "The Angel Guest and Other Poems and Lyrics."

1893 Dies at Kingston (December 9).

CHAPTER 1

The Formative Years

I *Who Is Charles Sangster?*

Charles Sangster is anything but a well-known literary figure. A pioneer among Canadian poets, he was greatly overrated when his work first appeared, but he has been all but ignored for almost a hundred years. He remains, however, the most important Canadian poet of his generation. And, unlike most of his contemporaries, he was neither an immigrant nor an emigrant. He was born in Canada; he lived all of his life in Canada; and he lies buried in Canada.

Sangster published two volumes of poetry: *The St. Lawrence and the Saguenay and Other Poems* (1856) and *Hesperus and Other Poems and Lyrics* (1860). He also contributed a number of poems and one criticial article to the Canadian periodicals of his time, and he issued one poem, "Our Norland," as a chapbook. Apart from a few otherwise unpublished poems which appeared in E. H. Dewart's *Selections from Canadian Poets* (1864), this constitutes his published work.[1] His two volumes were never reprinted, and they are available today only in a few larger libraries, where they are usually to be found in special, noncirculating collections. To most poetry readers, he is known only through the standard anthologies. His work has been represented (though not always judiciously) in every major anthology of Canadian poetry since Dewart's *Selections*—the first such publication.

In addition to Sangster's published work, there is a body of material in manuscript, which is now possessed by McGill University. In the following pages, this manuscript material is referred to as the McGill Collection, or simply as the manuscripts. The McGill Collection is composed principally of unpublished poetry, but it also contains manuscript versions of most of the poems which were published in periodicals, an autobiographical fragment, a group of fifteen letters which Sangster wrote to W. D. Lighthall between 1888 and 1893, one letter which he wrote to George J. Wilson in 1890, and a few miscellaneous items.

Apart from the letters in the McGill Collection, excerpts from which were quoted by Desmond Pacey in his *Ten Canadian Poets* (1958), there are four letters written to William Kirby between 1886 and 1891, all of which were reproduced by Lorne Pierce in his *William Kirby: The Portrait of a Tory Loyalist* (1929); three letters written to David Gibson between 1872 and 1883; and one letter written to George Stewart in 1886. Passages from letters written to E. H. Dewart in the 1860's were quoted by Dewart in his essays on Sangster, but the letters themselves no longer exist so far as is known.

Almost all of the published biographical sketches of Sangster are brief, and many of them contain inaccuracies. Desmond Pacey's essay in his *Ten Canadian Poets* represents the only serious attempt made to date to collate existing biographical material and present as complete an account as possible of the poet's life. The fact that Pacey was able to flesh his findings into a coherent narrative within a space of about twenty pages is indicative of the sorry state of the record. "It is improbable," says Pacey, "that a book-length biography will ever be written: the materials are simply not available."[2] The difficulty facing the biographer is that Sangster's existence was obscure. He never held an important position; he joined no movements; he belonged to no national associations (except, briefly, to the Royal Society of Canada); and he was on intimate terms with few prominent persons. Biographical research, therefore, demands the skills of the genealogist more than those of the literary critic.

In terms of factual content, the biographical account in this volume goes beyond any account previously published. This would have been possible merely by making more exhaustive use of the limited source materials on which other sketches (notably Pacey's) are based. Also, however, some lost items of information were retrieved from newspapers and magazines, and the letters to Gibson and Stewart and some other unpublished materials were located and used.[3] The barrenness of the biography is still painfully apparent, but if it is realized that even such an authoritative work as the latest edition of A. J. M. Smith's *Book of Canadian Poetry* contains a major error of biographical fact about Sangster, it may be better understood why this is so.[4]

II *Ancestry*

"My grandfather Sangster was, I believe, from Leith, Scotland. My grandfather on my mother's side (Ross) was from Ross-shire. . . . So I suppose the Scotch will, with some justice, lay claim to me; although my grandmother on my father's side was Irish, and my grandmother on my mother's side was English almost, for the Munros, from which she sprang, could scarcely have been English. So I have the blood of the three kingdoms in me—the greater part being Scottish."[5] So wrote Charles Sangster in a letter to the critic and anthologist E. H. Dewart in 1864. In his grandfather Sangster, the poet took a childlike pride.

Charles Sangster, my paternal grandfather, was a fiery old Scot from Fifeshire, and no man was better known as such in the Second Battalion, 60th Regiment, and subsequently in H.M.'s 44th Foot, than Sergeant Charles Sangster. He served his country for over thirty-one years, and served under General Burgoyne, passing through the entire first American Revolution. He is represented as having been brave as a lion, and of a quick and excitable disposition. His intense loyalty was proverbial. On one occasion, a picquet, of a Commissioned Officer, and a proper complement of non-Commissioned Officers, with my grandfather as the Sergeant, was surprised by a party of the Enemy. The Officer ran—a rare occurence in a British Army—and Sergeant Sangster took immediate charge of the party and brought them safely to the Camp; so there is some heroic blood in a Canadian Poet. For this act he was entitled to a Commission, which he would have obtained had he not preferred remaining in the colony.[6]

Following the revolution, Sergeant Sangster settled his family in Prince Edward Island, a colony which was rather extensively homesteaded in the 1780's by disbanded British soldiers and United Empire Loyalists—refugees from the revolutionary conflict to the south. It was claimed by the Sangster descendants that the Sergeant was married to an Irish woman, who bore him seven sons, but almost nothing is known, apart from what the poet tells us in the autobiographical fragment. Of the Sergeant's sons, we know only James, the poet's father, by name.

James Sangster would not have been born in Prince Edward Island, but he was probably quite a young child when his parents settled there, and he grew up and married on the island. His wife, Ann Ross, was a daughter of Hugh and Catherine Munro Ross, unusually literate, God-fearing immigrants from Scotland, who had also chosen to settle on the good farmland of Prince Edward Island. The original Ross family home was in the Cascumpeque Bay region, but the family later moved to Malpeque and, following her husband's death, Catherine lived with her son, John, in the Charlottetown area. So far as is known, there were only two children in the family: John and Ann.

"I think it was in 1802–3," wrote the poet, "that my parents left [Prince Edward Island], proceeding upward to Canada." Maybe it was later than 1803, because in that year Ann would have been only about fourteen years of age, but it is evident from the Ross letters that James and Ann Sangster had indeed left the island by 1806.[7] The earliest letter in this interesting collection was written by Hugh Ross, to his "children," James and Ann Sangster, on July 9, 1809, and in it he complains that his daughter and son-in-law have been "careless and indifferent" in not writing in more than three years. He wrote to them, he states, on June 30, 1806, and again on June 30, 1807. Having received no reply, he decided not to write in 1808, but now he "must break the silence" because he and Mrs. Ross are "very uneasy concerning your welfare." It is evident from this letter that James and Ann left the island in some haste and against the advice of Ann's parents. Hugh Ross says: "I believe you might have done better had you remained here but I left that entirely to your own discretion, only I wish that you have not repented your hurried flight from home." The parents' kindness and goodwill is unfaltering. "Your mother had some butter," he states, "and yarn for stockings and mittens and other things ready to send ... but we had no opportunity. ... May the Almighty God bless you all. So prays your loving father and mother."

James and Ann Sangster probably lived at Quebec City for a number of years before settling permanently at Kingston, Upper Canada. There is really no proof of this, apaxt from Catherine Ross's mention, in one of her letters to her daughter, of a person "you met in Quebec," but we also know from the Ross letters that they were at a city in the Canadas where soldiers were garrisoned, and since James was a shipwright, we may assume that they were also at a shipbuilding center. The following letter of Catherine Ross's leaves no doubt that James and Ann are living in Kingston in 1814, but it also reveals that they have moved there quite recently. In this letter, Catherine tells of Hugh Ross's death and of her profound desire to have her wandering daughter come home.

WEST RIVER, PRINCE EDWARD ISLAND
26th Oct., 1814

DEAR SON & DAUGHTER,

I take this opportunity to inform you how we are. Blessed be the Lord for his mercies we are in health. I am sorry to inform you of your father's death, but the Lord's will must be done. Your father took sick last Sept. and he was on his death bed twenty-four days. ... We tried at the Doctors that was in the Island, and it was all in vain. ...

We heard by the last soldiers that came to this Island from Canada that you went to Kingston and we are very much surprised at you for not writing to us this two years past. I wish you would write to me what family you have got and what way you are. ... There is nothing in the world that would give me more pleasure than if you could come to this Island if it is possible that you could do it, for we are left lonesome here. ... If you would come your Husband would get work in Charlotte

Town every day in the year. There is nothing upon earth that would give me more pleasure than to see you here about me in my old days. . . .

Your loving Mother,
CATHERINE ROSS

In April, 1815, Ann Sangster wrote to her mother to say that she might revisit the island during the summer, and in her reply, dated May 29, 1815, her mother again urged: "There is nothing in this world that would give me so much pleasure as to see you both here." This was probably Catherine Ross's last letter to her daughter, because she soon became a helpless invalid and a burden to her son, John, for the remainder of her life. She was still living in 1835.

Sangster claims in the autobiographical fragment that his grandfather, Sergeant Charles Sangster, was a Loyalist and that James Sangster, as the son of a Loyalist, was entitled to a free land grant. There is actually no proof that the Sangsters were classed as Loyalists, but James did receive a grant of land in Kingston by Order-in-Council dated September 4, 1822, "on the same Conditions as a Military Claimant."[8] James was employed with the Navy Department while he lived in Kingston (and probably from the time he left Prince Edward Island). In such documents as his name appears, he is designated as a "joiner," "shipwright," or "shipbuilder." Although he was based at Kingston, he was required by the Navy Department to move from port to port on the Great Lakes. Responsibility for raising the children was, therefore, left almost entirely with his wife, Ann, from the start. By July, 1822, there were four surviving children—Hugh, James, John, and Catherine—and the birth of a fifth child was being awaited.

III *Kingston and the First Years*

Had Sangster been able to choose the place of his birth and upbringing, he could hardly have picked a more favorable spot than Kingston in the Canada of the 1820's. Situated where Lake Ontario empties into the Saint Lawrence River, Kingston is amid natural surroundings of unusual variety and beauty. The great lake, the Thousand Islands, the Saint Lawrence and Cataraqui rivers, colorful rural countryside, and endless forest spelled an almost ideal physical environment for an embryo nature poet. Relative to the rawness of most other Canadian towns and cities, the town of Kingston itself, with its clean limestone buildings, was a dignified and graceful place to live in the early nineteenth century, and it was at that time, moreover, one of the largest and most important commercial and military centers in Canada.

By the 1820's Kingston already had a proud history—first as an Indian settlement called Cadaracqui, then as the site of France's Fort Frontenac, and finally as a permanent settlement founded by a migration of New York state Loyalists in 1783. In 1792, when the first meeting of the Executive Council of Upper Canada was held, it was held at Kingston, which was by then the principal town in what was later to become the province of Ontario. As the base of the British naval establishment on Lake Ontario and as a key communications and transportation center, Kingston figured prominently in the War of 1812, and for the protection of the Naval Dockyard, construction of Fort Henry, the strongest military post west of Quebec, was begun in 1813.

In 1800 Kingston had only about five hundred inhabitants, but by 1824 the population had grown to over two thousand, to place Kingston third (behind Quebec City and Montreal) among Canadian centers of population. The 1820's were boom times in Kingston. The Rideau Canal linking Kingston with Ottawa was begun, and bridges, public buildings, and churches were erected. The town was already served by two newspapers and a theater, and it had a flourishing social life, as the following item from an early newspaper report suggests: "Mr. John Glover, His Majesty's Naval Storekeeper, invited fifty ladies and gentlemen of fashion to take wine with him on H.M.S. *Bullfrog*."[9]

There was also a squalid side to the Kingston of the 1820's. Pigs, geese, dogs, and cats ran wild in the muddy streets. Alcoholism was widespread among the population, and rowdiness and violence were rampant. Taverns remained open on Sundays "for the reception of the vile and dissolute of both sexes, and that in the most barefaced and shameful manner."[10] The laws of the time were harsh and the punishments severe. Whipping posts and stocks were still in use, and men were frequently hanged for such offenses as horse stealing or cattle rustling. Public hangings were in style and were occasions of high merriment. On such days, the roads leading to Kingston would be crowded from early morning. At the scene would be found parents with their children, young men with their sweethearts, and an unruly mob smoking, drinking, gambling, and quarreling, while the execution hour was awaited.

It was into this setting that Charles Sangster was born on July 16, 1822. He was not actually born within the town of Kingston; his parents lived at the Navy Yard, or rather on the outskirts of the premises known by that name, at Point Frederick, opposite the town. A twin sister, who died in infancy, was born with him. At the time of his birth, a cholera was afoot in Upper Canada. His uncle John Ross, in Prince Edward Island, expressed his concern over this in a letter to his sister, dated September 8, 1822: "I would like to be more fully satisfied concerning it," he wrote, "whether you had it in your family, or whether it is gone out of the country." We know that the Sangsters somehow survived this epidemic, but apart from John Ross's letter, there is an eighteen-month silence in the record following Charles's birth.

In the winter of 1824, James Sangster was stationed at Fort William. On January 22 he wrote to his wife, stating that he was in good health, urging her to write to him, and passing the following simple, fatherly messages on to his children: "Lett me no [about] James and Hugh and give my kind love to them hoping they will be kind and dutiful to their mother during my absence. Tell Kitty that tho Father often scolded her it was not becose he did not like her for if she was along with me she would mend and wash but here I have to dow it myself. . . . Tell John Father hopes he will be a good boy and mind to be kind and obedient to his mother and I will be good to him accordingley. Tell my littel twin Charles that Father oftin thinks on him and you must kiss him for me."[11]

Six months later, James was stationed at Penetanguishene, on Georgian Bay. From there, on July 30, he sent this moving last letter to his wife, Ann. The contrast in style and spelling between the January letter and this letter of July 30 suggests that he required assistance with this one:

DEAR WIFE,
I received your letter today and was sorry to find by it that you and the Family have been so unwell. I have requested Bayfield to transmit you an advance of money on my account. I have been severely indisposed. I am in the greatest state of debility; but keep up your spirits, and place your sole dependence upon God, whom I trust will be a Father to my children, and will help you out in all your difficulties in this life. Accept my best wishes, and remember me to [name illegible], not forgetting poor little Charles.
I remain,

Your affect. Husband,
JAMES SANGSTER[12]

He did not recover.

IV *Schooling*

"My mother," Sangster wrote, "was left with a large family when my father died, I being the youngest. Having to work hard to maintain her family by the labor of her hands, it is not to be wondered at that I have not had the benefit of a classical education. But I remember having gone to several schoolmasters, who spoke most execrable English, and from whom I *didn't* learn to write my native tongue." It is not clear for what period of time Sangster attended school or exactly what he learned there. Most biographical sketches state that he left school at fifteen, but this would seem to be an assumption based on his claim (in the autobiographical fragment) that he "left home" at fifteen. In the autobiographical fragment, he says that he went to school for "many years" and "learned to read and write, if nothing more." He has "pleasant recollections," he says, of three of his teachers: "two Irishmen—and another, worse than either, who might have been from the Hill of Howth, Yorkshire, or Tipperary, so far as his pronunciation was concerned."

In his letter of February 1, 1883, to his friend David Gibson (a Kingston merchant), Sangster reveals that one of the schools he attended was called Ross's Lancashire School, and he also reveals that, even in his old age, he has not forgiven "gentleman Ross" or the schools generally for promoting a curriculum based on Latin and Greek:

I remember Johnny Harkness learning, or trying to learn some of the dead languages at Ross' Lancashire School, where he and I—and a good many other brilliants—went once upon a time. Johnny used to hold his book behind his back with a forefinger thrust in at the lesson page, and he regularly turned round to take a glance at it every time gentleman Ross, who promenaded up and down, passed him, and facing round suddenly very innocent and lamblike, as gentleman Ross right about faced on his way back; and so on to the end of the Latin lesson. Considering what a delicious dunce Johnny was these very dead languages must have had the dreary effect of deadening his faculties for all time to come.

The only mention of school in the poetry is in the poem "Pleasant Memories" in *The St. Lawrence and the Saguenay*, but once again the memory is not altogether pleasant:

> Do you remember the old school-room
> That seemed little else than a solemn tomb?
>   Though on looking back
>   On life's beaten track,
> Those hours were happier far than they seemed,
> Dearer than ever we thought or dreamed!

Fragmentary though the evidence is, it is quite clear that Sangster found the school curriculum irrelevant and his masters stern and uninspiring. His school experiences probably helped to engender the strain of anti-intellectualism which runs through his poetry. When we reflect upon the vital role performed by good teachers in lighting the imaginations of so many of

Canada's poets and in assisting them also in practical ways, we appreciate that Sangster's failure to find an interested and sympathetic schoolmaster may have been one of the gravest misfortunes of his life. We think of George R. Parkin, the great schoolmaster at the Fredericton Collegiate, who brought the dead languages to life for a generation of poets and writers of the Roberts and Carman families, or of Hugh MacLennan's classics master at the old Halifax Academy who taught the embryo novelist "respect for life—not life as it might be, not life as it ought to be, but life as it is."[13] Poor Sangster, by contrast, seems to have been shown a picture only of what life never was and never would become.

Sangster sat alone in his log hut of learning, with no Mark Hopkins on the other end of the bench. "All that I possess mentally," he says, in the autobiographical fragment, "has been acquired by careful reading of the best authors (chiefly fiction), properly directed thought, and a tolerable share of industry." This self-education did not take place in childhood, however. "I would have read more in my younger days," he says, "but books were not to be had—the *Bible*, and the *Citizen of the World* in two volumes constituted my library for many years. Until the cheap publishing system was adopted I had little to read. I remember having a grand feast over the tragedy of *Macbeth* and *Elizabeth, or the Exiles in Siberia.* There was no *Sanford and Merton*, no *Arabian Nights*, no *Robinson Crusoe* for me until I had attained maturity." A lending library (surely one of the first in Canada) opened in Kingston in 1804, but the Sangster family would probably not have been able to pay the substantial subscription fees. And the rigid class distinctions observed in a city dominated by military officers probably denied Sangster access, as a child, to the homes of citizens with private libraries. These are moot points. All that we know for certain, apart from what Sangster makes explicit in the autobiographical fragment and in his letters, is that, as an adult, he was widely read in poetry, and especially so in the Romantic and early Victorian periods. His brain was freighted with the cadences, and too often with the phrases, of a score of poets, major and minor, English and American.

V *A Job at Fort Henry*

The viability of the household of the widow Sangster at Point Frederick, Kingston, depended for many years upon the willingness and capacity of the sons and daughter to help, and some of the problems which Mrs. Sangster had in this regard are revealed to us in letters which she received from her brother John in the 1830's. From John's letter of October 24, 1830, for example, we learn that James, the second son, was somehow severely injured and completely disabled and that he lingered, it would seem, between life and death for several years. In his letter of May 28, 1832, John Ross acknowledges having received word of James's death and in the same letter expresses his displeasure at having heard that Catherine has left home. "She was young enough," he says, "and might wait a while yet." Hugh, the eldest son, would seem to have married in the early 1830's. In his letter of May 28, 1835, John Ross states: "I am happy to understand that Hugh and his child are recovered and doing well—likewise to hear that John is so near out of his time. . . . He and Charles are the only two that are near you of all your family, therefore I trust they will not forget you in your latter days." Hugh Sangster eventually settled in Buffalo, New York, and John Sangster in his own home in Kingston. Both men became tinsmiths.

It is probable that both Hugh and John Sangster had left their mother's home by 1837. In any case, in that year, when the Canadas were seething with unrest, Charles Sangster, age fifteen, went to work to help support his widowed mother. His first job was with the Ordnance Department at the newly constructed and recently garrisoned Fort Henry, where life was exciting at the time, if not always pleasant.

The Rebellion of 1837, in Upper and Lower Canada, was aimed at seizing for the elected legislative assemblies of the provinces important powers still held by the nominated legislative councils. A plan by the fugitive leader, Mackenzie, to seize Fort Henry in the winter of 1838 with an American force of two thousand men did not materialize. However, in the same year, a young Polish American, Nils von Schultz, a gentleman of noble birth and liberal education, was deluded by certain of Mackenzie's followers into believing that Upper Canadians were under the heel of a merciless tyranny; and, acting solely from principle, he led an invasion force of one hundred and sixty adventurers across the Saint Lawrence River at Prescott. After the four-day Battle of the Windmill, "General" von Schultz was captured by a force from Kingston and was taken to Fort Henry for trial by court-martial. No doubt Sangster, who helped make the cartridges used in the battle, witnessed the proud young Pole being marched through the midnight streets of Kingston at the head of his tattered troops. Said Sangster: "I might have seen the brave, but misguided Pole, Von Schultz, hanged on the Glacis at Fort Henry, but did not, as I considered then, as I do now, that the instigators of the insurrection, men who still hold up their heads in Canada, deserved that fate a thousand times more than the heroic foreigner who was made a sacrifice to their rebellious acts."

In 1839 Sangster was transferred from his menial task at the laboratory at Fort Henry to the Ordnance Office—where he labored for ten years for a promotion which never came:

From the laboratory I was removed to the Ordnance Office, where I ranked as a messenger, received the pay of a labourer, and did the duty of a clerk. This is too frequently the case in public departments; the favoured ones who have interest at Court coming in for all the promotion. This lasted for ten years; but no advancement. There *was* a chance of promotion (a mere Foremanship) for which I was recommended to the Power by the late James Sutton Elliott, Esq., then Ordnance Commissioner . . . but through the interference of Mr. Windsor, then Ordnance Storekeeper at Kingston, I failed to obtain the situation. I was of more use to him in a subordinate capacity. I left the department in the summer of 1849, having lost ten of the best years of my life pursuing a myth.

The year was 1849; Sangster was twenty-seven.

"Even as a boy," said Sangster, "my ear seems to have been tuned to the harmony of sounds. . . . I began to write for the newspapers, laying the foundations of *The St. Lawrence and the Saguenay* and *Hesperus*." Since most of the verse which appeared in the Kingston newspapers in the 1830's and 1840's appeared anonymously or pseudonymously, Sangster's earliest ventures in verse could not easily be unearthed.[14] However, while he was at the Ordnance Office, he gave much of his spare time to working in the office of the *British Whig*, and it was during this period certainly that he began to write in earnest.

The earliest dated poem which we have belongs to the period when he was filling cartridges at Fort Henry. The poem, entitled "The Rebel," is discussed in Chapter 6, but it is interesting from the biographical standpoint as well. The subject of the poem is the Rebellion of 1837, and from it we learn, if we did not already know from his comments on Von Schultz's execution, that Sangster had no sympathy with Mackenzie's cause. In fact, in "The Rebel," he displays contempt both for the principles advanced by the rebels and for Mackenzie personally, whom he regarded as a base coward. From "The Rebel" too we learn that, at the age of seventeen, Sangster had already gone a long way toward acquiring the poetic vocabulary which was to serve him throughout his career, and that he had already found his themes—at least his themes of nature and love.

Having left his uncongenial job with the Fort Henry Ordnance Department a discouraged and somewhat embittered man, Sangster must have been pleased to obtain, in the summer of 1849, the editorship of the

Courier, of Amhertsburg, Canada West, even though the paper was but a small-town weekly. This particular move served him to no avail, however, as the *Courier's* publisher, a Mr. Reeves, died in the fall of 1849. The paper promptly ceased publication, and Sangster was again out of a job. He returned to Kingston and in the spring of 1850 obtained a position with the *British Whig*, where he had had experience in a part-time capacity in the 1840's. His title with the *Whig* was subeditor, but his duties were those of a bookkeeper and proofreader. The work was demanding and not very agreeable to one whose imagination was given to flights of fancy, but the fact is that the years which he spent with the *Whig* were by far and away his most productive years as a poet.

CHAPTER 2

The Productive Years

I *Volume One and Marriage*

During its thirteen-year existence, the *Literary Garland*, Canada's first successful literary magazine, counted among its contributors such distinguished Canadian writers as Susannah Moodie, Catherine Parr Traill, Mrs. Anna Jameson, Mrs. Leprohon, and Maj. John Richardson. Although it definitely encouraged native talent and published contributions from the most uncompromising of early nineteenth-century Canadian writers, the *Garland* was essentially a genteel publication, in the manner of most of the East Coast American literary journals of the time. As a palliative to the rawness of colonial life, it offered to its readers a polite, effeminate world where blushing maidens, sentimentality, class snobbery, and religious propriety ruled supreme.

Charles Sangster made his national literary debut in the December, 1850, issue of the *Literary Garland*, with two innocuous little verses entitled "Bright Eyes" and "The Orphan Girl." Here is a sample stanza from each of these poems:

> Indulgent heaven
> Has strangely given
> To woman, the two-fold power,
> To ease the heart
> Or to fix the dart,
> With a *look* in affliction's hour!

> .   .   .   .

> She was a tender little child,
>   That orphan Girl that trod the plain,
> Where Winter's sternest sprites beguiled
>   The time, and fell in drizzling rain;
> Upon her neck, benumbed and bare
> Hung her half-stiffened locks of hair,
> In dripping tresses, floating wild,
> Sending a chill through every vein.

Verse of this sort suited the tastes and purposes of the *Garland's* editors but, happy to say, Sangster himself was discriminating enough not to include these particular pieces in his published collections. "The Recluse," a lengthier descriptive lyric, appeared in the January, 1851, issue of the *Garland*. The poem has moments of rhythmic power, but it is thoroughly conventional in thought and diction, and Sangster chose to exclude it too from his published volumes.

Successor to the *Garland*, as Canada's leading literary magazine, was the *Anglo-American Magazine*, which began publication in 1852. Like so many other publishers in Canadian history, Thomas Maclear of the *Anglo-American* soon encountered grave financial difficulties, and the magazine ceased publication in 1855. Just as Sangster had been featured in the dying numbers of the *Garland*, so was he also in the last issues of the *Anglo-American*, but this time, rather than contributing verses to suit the style and tone of the journal, he made an effort to prepare the way for his forthcoming first volume by submitting samples of his best work. The July, 1855, issue of the *Anglo-American* must have been a welcome one to Canadian poetry enthusiasts because it contained (under the title "A 'Thousand Island' Lyric") Sangster's excellent "Lyric to the Isles" from the title poem of *The St. Lawrence and the Saguenay*. He contributed another poem to the August, 1855, number of the *Anglo-American*, but at this time, as he was on the threshold of bolder initiatives, both personal and literary, he disappeared from the pages of the journals for a period of eight years.

While the manuscript of his first book was in the hands of the printer, Charles Sangster, age thirty-four, was preparing to marry Mary Kilborn, age twenty-one. Mary was the "fourth daughter" of William Henry Kilborn, Colborn Street, Kingston, a deputy provincial land surveyor, a long-time resident of the city, and a man held in some esteem. The marriage took place on September 16, 1856, at Saint James's Anglican Church, Kingston.[1]

The St. Lawrence and the Saguenay and Other Poems, dated June, 1856, was published by subscription through the firm of Miller, Orton, and Mulligan, of Auburn, New York. It was dedicated to John Sinclair, a "friend and correspondent of many years," whose identity, beyond that, resides in the oblivion into which all but the highlights of Sangster's life has fallen. It is two hundred and sixty-two pages in length and contains eighty-two poems (including a major title poem). Throughout the book, Sangster shows himself to be a sincere lover of the natural world. He is awed by the immensity of creation and the seeming omnipotence of natural forces, and his senses are receptive to the sights and sounds of nature. The tint and texture of the granite, the motion of the buttercup as it opens its petals to the sun, and the weirdness of the lamb's bleat from a distant hillside do not escape his notice. He also shows himself to be a man enraptured by love to the point that he frequently fails to achieve objectivity in his love poems. On the other hand, he leaves no doubt about the fact that he is subject to moods of profound, and sometimes morbid, melancholy. There is little sign of youthfulness or gaiety, and there is no hint whatever of rebelliousness or recklessness in the image which this volume projects of the poet. Regardless of his subject or his mood, he is always both intensely serious and deeply religious. Here, one feels, is a man who keeps to the straight and narrow through faith in a personal God and strict adherence to moral principle.

Critical response to *The St. Lawrence and the Saguenay* was not only favorable, but indiscriminately so—in Canada, the United States, and Great Britain.[2] Sangster's own newspaper, the *Whig*, stated that the volume was "a credit to Canadian Literature." The rival Kingston *News* said: "We hail this contributor to the scanty store of Canadian Literature, and we congratulate Kingston in having in its midst one possessed of potential talent in so high a degree." The Kingston *Commercial Advertiser* viewed the volume in a moral light:

What we most admire in Mr. Sangster is his warm and ardent love for the beautiful and the good, and his never-failing charity; that he possesses poetical talent in a high degree anyone capable of judging will allow. His reverence of the God-like, his love of the beautiful, his adoration of the true, commend his first breathings in the world of authorship to every right-thinker.

The small-town press of Canada West drew two conclusions: the poetry was Canadian, and the poet was without peer in Canada:

We hail the publication of these poems, to which we readily invite attention. They are chiefly upon topics incidental to British America; betray considerable talent, and no slight poetic skill and taste, while to their good feeling and admirable tone we give our warmest testimony. —Canadian (London) *News*

Mr. Sangster is a poet of no mean order, and his volume is far the most respectable contribution of Poetry that has yet been made to the infant literature of Canada. —Huron *Signal*

These Poems as a whole are every way worthy of the Genius of a true-born poet like Mr. Sangster, our Native Bard; the public may well afford to patronize the best the country has produced. —Hamilton *Spectator*

[29]

The statements of the reviewers in Ottawa, Toronto, and Montreal were only somewhat less definitive:

These poems are written in a bold masterly style, full of imagery, and displaying ability of no ordinary kind. Mr. Sangster is a Poet, in the true sense of the term, and leads his readers in burning language of inspiration from Nature up to Nature's God. —Ottawa *Times*

Mr. Sangster possesses a lively imagination, united to good descriptive powers, and is likely to make himself widely known as a genuine friend of the Muses. —Toronto *Globe*

This is a book that, as a Canadian, we are proud of. The subject upon which it treats is one well worthy of the high talents of the Author. We are glad the volume has been published; it is a great addition to the literary products of the province. To tourists it is indispensable. As they pass along on their tour of pleasure over these two rivers, it would be a treat to read his chaste and classic muse. —Montreal *Pilot*

In the United States, the Buffalo *Republic* described Sangster as "a writer who will yet make his mark in the literary world," and generally speaking, reviews published south of the border were no less laudatory than those in Canadian journals. The New York *Albion* said "Mr. Sangster is something more than one of the mob of gentlemen who write with ease. We should be glad to hear from him again." In 1856, however, the judgments which really mattered were not rendered either in Canada or the United States, but in Great Britain, where, as one writer of the time sarcastically put it, reviewers "could naturally expect very little excellence to come out of Canada, or any other of the colonial Nazareths," and had the usual custom of demolishing Canadian books "for mere recreation." But Sangster's volume was very well received, the London *National Magazine* going so far as to describe him as "the Wordsworth of Canada":

Western Canada is enabled to boast, and does boast somewhat loudly, of Charles Sangster, who has celebrated in Spenserian Stanzas the beauties and the sublimities of the St. Lawrence and the Saguenay. Well may Canadians be proud of such contributions to their infant literature; well may they be forward to recognize his lively imagination, his bold masterly style. and the fulness of his imagery. . . . There is much of the spirit of Wordsworth in this writer, only the tone is religious instead of being philosophical. . . . In some sort, and according to his degree, he may be regarded as the Wordsworth of Canada.

Sangster was sufficiently interested in the reviews to keep them and to publish excerpts from them in an appendix to his second volume. It is interesting that he headed the collection of reviews not with statements made by the *National Magazine*, but with this congratulatory letter which he received from another Canadian writer:

BELLEVILLE, July 28th, 1856.

SIR—Accept my sincere thanks for the volume of beautiful Poems with which you have favored me. If the world receives them with as much pleasure as they have been read by me, your name will rank high among the gifted Sons of Song. If a native of Canada, she may well be proud of her Bard, who has sung in such lofty strains the natural beauties of his native land. Wishing you all the fame you so richly deserve, I subscribe myself, your sincere admirer.

SUSANNA MOODIE.

If Sangster was at all dizzied by this reception, there is no evidence of it. Throughout his life, it would seem that he remained constant both in his capacity for detachment from the passing scene and in his capacity for self-criticism. Many of the poems in *The St. Lawrence and the Saguenay*, he soon became convinced, should never have been published, and he set about immediately to prepare a second volume with which he himself would be better satisfied.

II *Tragedy and Turmoil*

If 1856 was a shining summit in Charles Sangster's life, 1858 was one of many dark valleys. On December 3, 1857, his father-in-law, William H. Kilborn, died suddenly at the age of fifty-nine, and the family did not have time to recover before fate dealt an even crueler blow. Mary Kilborn, the poet's wife of less than eighteen months, contracted pneumonia soon after her father's death and fell victim to it on January 18, 1858. The Kingston *Daily News* of January 20 carried the austere notice:

DIED—In Kingston, on the 18th January, instant, Mary Kilborn, wife of Mr. Charles Sangster, of that city, aged 22 years and 9 months. Friends and acquaintances are invited to attend the funeral of the deceased, without further notice, at Mr. Sangster's residence, Barrie Street, this (Wednesday) afternoon at three o'clock, to the cemetery at Waterloo.

This was only the first of a series of personal tragedies which punctuated Sangster's middle and later years. His poetic excursions in the realms of melancholy and remorse are not simply romantic exercises. Though we must, as mere literary observers, rap his knuckles for the subjectivity and sentimentality of much of this poetry of sorrow, it is, in the biographical context, often strikingly restrained. Writing several years later of the death of his youthful and adored Mary, Sangster quoted Shelley as saying that "Poets learn in suffering what they teach in song." In this respect, at least, he would not be able to complain that his education was defective.

It is reasonable to assume that the death of his wife robbed Sangster for a time of a sense of purpose and direction and that this may have prompted his decision to undergo a phrenological examination in 1859. The "Phrenological Character of Mr. Charles Sangster, Given at Fowler and Wells Phrenological Cabinet, Number 308 Broadway, New York, by L. N. Fowler, Professor of Phrenology, October Eighteenth, 1859" is now in the McGill Collection. Although it is the product of a discredited science, the "Character" is the only commentary of its kind which we have on the poet at this important period in his life. In it we are given a picture of a man not well equipped to "buffet with the world or take the rough-and-tumble of life," one who cannot adapt himself well to the "plain, common duties and business of the day," but one who is highly principled, highly sensitive, and warmhearted. "You are a genius in your way," states the phrenologist, "you have great versatility of mind . . . you use language correctly and copiously . . . you have a correct eye . . . as an artist." The poetry and the fragmentary records of Sangster's existence stand as a testimonial to the truth of these observations and many others made in the phrenologist's report, and there is nothing of a contradictory nature in the "Character."

Was Sangster, as the phrenologist reports, also reserved, fearful of accidents, and delicate in his choice of food and drink? And did he give the impression of being haughty and proud? These and other characteristics mentioned by the phrenologist seem to square very well with what we do know, and to be realistic we must surely allow that the written reports of successful professional phrenologists were probably based as much on close observation of the client and good practical judgment as they were on cranial measurements. In any case, Sangster valued his "Character" and desired that it be kept for posterity. Only nine months before his death, when he was putting his papers in order for safekeeping, he mailed it to W. D. Lighthall with a request that it be placed among his notes and manuscripts.

In spite of the tragedy and turmoil of the 1850's, the decade ended well. By 1860 Sangster's physical and creative energies were at their apex, and he was prepared to risk both another marriage and the publication of a second volume of verse.

III   *Volume Two and Remarriage*

Sangster's second wife was Henrietta Charlotte Mary Meagher, a daughter of Dr. James Meagher, a Kingston physician, and his wife, Katherine Robertson Clemow. The marriage took place at Niagara Falls on October 23, 1860.[3] While it would be difficult to believe that sad and saintly Charles Sangster cut a very dashing figure in Kingston in the 1850's, it is nevertheless a fact that at least two very young ladies found him to be an irresistible suitor. He was thirty-eight years old when he married Henrietta Meagher; she was only seventeen. "Let us hope," wrote Sangster of himself, "that he will have a larger lease of domestic happiness and companionship than fell to his lot by his first marriage." He may have had his wish, because it was a modest one, but there was more domestic tragedy to come, and the tradition has come down in Kingston that the second marriage was not a happy one.[4]

Hesperus and Other Poems and Lyrics was published in 1860 at Sangster's personal expense through Montreal publisher John Lovell, who had been the publisher of the *Literary Garland*, to which Sangster had been a contributor. Smaller than the first volume and containing poems more carefully selected and more highly perfected, *Hesperus* brought its author even more spectacular praise than had *The St. Lawrence and the Saguenay*.[5] Here are sample comments from three Canadian newspapers:

The easy grace and finish of some of his lyrics would be creditable to the genius of Moore. . . . More than his first book, *Hesperus* commends itself to the people. —Kingston *Daily News*.

We have one worthy of the name of poet among us. —Montreal *Transcript*.

Mr. Sangster, himself a most ethereal being, has refined, subliminated, and crystalized, by the force of his genius, the objects of his poetic admiration. . . . It certainly speaks and augurs badly for the future of this country, that its sons of talent and genius must be tried at the bar of British criticism. . . . Let Canada wipe this stigma from her literature. —Woodstock *Times*

As the following passage reveals, Sangster had nothing to fear from "the bar of British criticism":

In this volume there is an undoubted facility, while there is a great variety of versification. There is much sincere appreciation of the beauties of poetical phraseology, best descriptive of forests, lakes, rivers, moonlight nights, and starry skies. . . . Beside such poets as Coventry Patmore and Charles Mackay, he may claim a place without any presumption. —Glasgow *Commonwealth.*

When *The St. Lawrence and the Saguenay* was published, the New York *Albion* recognized in Sangster "the germ of a future poet." Reminding readers of this the *Albion* crowned him in a lengthy review of *Hesperus*:

Charles Sangster is now, we think, fairly entitled to a place on "Parnassus' Hill" . . . . Love, as we poor mortals know it, is his frequent theme. The domestic affections prompt him. In rural life he revels. His patriotism glows.

Bayard Taylor wrote Sangster approvingly and expressed the hope that he would "give us many more corner stones [as] there is quite a mine of poetic wealth in Canada, if it were properly worked." Few comments could have pleased Sangster more than those of the master of the breakfast table. "His verse," wrote Oliver Wendell Holmes, "adds new interest to the woods and streams amidst which he sings and embellishes the charms of the maidens he celebrates."[6] "The New York *Albion*," said Sangster (with less than his usual modesty), "and other reliable authorities elevate me to the distinction of a poet, the first thorough Canadian who has yet attained to so high an honour in this elevated and difficult department of literature."

IV *The 1860's*

On April 18, 1863, Sangster's mother, Ann Sangster, who had been a widow for forty-one years, died at Point Frederick, Kingston, at the age of seventy-three.[7] Sangster was corresponding with E. H. Dewart at this time about the representation of his work in Dewart's forthcoming anthology, *Selections From Canadian Poets*. Sangster was very disturbed, Dewart later stated, over the death of his mother, but as usual, he was able to find solace in his unflagging religious faith. "There are gains for all our losses," he wrote to Dewart, "and while in this vein, I may say, referring to the closing paragraph of your letter, that, were it not for that 'other world,' 'the undiscovered country from whose bourne no traveller returns,' I should be the most miserable of mortals."

Sangster's chief literary activity in the early 1860's was the preparation of a revised edition of *The St. Lawrence and the Saguenay*. The revision of the title poem was completed by 1862, and by 1865 he had plans to publish the volume. (These plans, which were never realized, are discussed at some length in Chapter 6.) During its two-year existence, the *British American Magazine*, one of the most interesting periodicals of the period, featured prose and verse by many of the leading Canadian literary figures, including Charles Sangster, who published three new poems in the *British American* in 1863—one in each of the May, July, and October issues. In his *Selections from Canadian Poets* (1864), E. H. Dewart included no fewer than thirteen pieces from Sangster's published volumes, as well as three previously unpublished poems; in his introductory essay he assigned Sangster "first place among Canadian poets." Sangster published only one other poem in 1864. To celebrate William Cullen Bryant's seventieth birthday (November 3, 1864), the Century Club of New York sponsored a "Bryant Festival." Sangster wrote his poem "Bryant" for this occasion, and it was included in a commemorative volume issued by the club.[8] This much we know about his literary activity, but there is some confusion about how he earned his living during the early 1860's.

It will be recalled that throughout the 1850's he was with the Kingston *British Whig*, nominally as subeditor but actually as bookkeeper and proofreader. When and why he left the *Whig* is not clear. In his *Bibliotheca Canadensis* (1867), H. J. Morgan stated that Sangster remained with the *Whig* "during the best part of his life, until 1861." In his article on Sangster, published in 1869, George Stewart said that Sangster remained with the *Whig* "for eleven years," but Stewart may have made this calculation from Morgan's statement. Subsequent biographical sketches have sometimes repeated that he left the *Whig* in 1861. The sketches are unanimous in stating that he joined the Kingston *Daily News* in 1864 (in February, specifically) as a reporter. Sangster himself makes no mention of the move, either in the autobiographical fragment or in his letters. If, in fact, he left the *Whig* three years before he joined the *News*, there is a gap in his employment for which we have no explanation.

In 1865, Sangster began contributing to the *Saturday Reader*, of Montreal. He was welcomed with editorial enthusiasm to the columns of the new paper, and a highly favorable review of *Hesperus*, taken from the Dumphries *Observer* (Scotland), appeared in the January 20, 1866, issue. Altogether, two new poems and two revisions were featured, but then Sangster disappeared quietly from the *Reader* early in 1866, not to be heard from again, although the publication survived until 1870. Apart from one other minor poem, "McEachran," which appeared in the Kingston *Chronicle and News* (June 15, 1866), he did not publish anything else for more than two years.

On July 1, 1867, the British North America Act created the modern nation of Canada, although Canada was composed at first only of the former Canadas (East and West) and the two Maritime provinces of New Brunswick and Nova Scotia. Confederation was a dream come true for Sangster, who had championed the concept of a single, unified British North American nation in verse for at least a decade. The trials of his personal existence were not assuaged, however, by the provisions of the British North America Act. Lorne Pierce states in his biography of William Kirby that Sangster was corresponding with the novelist about this time and that he frequently spoke of the "depressing mental and monetary conditions of his life." His health was in a somewhat more precarious state than the phrase "depressing mental condition" would suggest. He was, in fact, in the grip of a nervous disorder of some sort which was to plague him for the rest of his life. Details about his illness are scarce, but we do know that in the late 1860's concern was being expressed over the prospects for his complete recovery. So far as his monetary impoverishment was concerned, hope finally broke in 1868 in the form of the offer of a clerkship in the new federal Post Office Department, in Ottawa.

Sangster has little to say himself on the subject, but the offer of the clerkship in Ottawa was interpreted by some as an act of recognition on the part of the new country of the importance of his artistic achievements. There is no evidence to show that his fellow Kingstonian, John A. Macdonald, Canada's first prime minister, ever took a personal interest in him. Wallace H. Robb, himself a Kingston poet versed in local history and folklore, says that, as far as he could discover, Macdonald's attitude toward Sangster was "nasty."[9] Be that as it may, Alexander Campbell, Macdonald's law partner for many years in Kingston, was postmaster general in MacDonald's first cabinet, and it was he who "nominated" Sangster for the position, in his own department. Campbell was a man of generous instincts, and the offer of the position, probably in response to a request from Sangster, was doubtless a small, personal act of patronage on his part rather than anything as grand as a national gesture. In any case, the position was such a minor one that it would have been disgraceful for the federal cabinet to regard it as an appropriate honor or reward to bestow upon the country's leading poet. The salary was five hundred dollars a year, and the duties were those of a "senior second class clerk."[10] With some misgivings, we may suppose, Sangster decided to accept the offer and move away from the city in which he had lived all of his forty-six years. He reported for duty in Ottawa on March 20, 1868.

No sooner had he arrived in Ottawa than domestic tragedy struck again. His daughter, Charlotte Mary, who was just over three years of age, contracted diphtheria, and died on April 6, 1868. When his first wife died, he succeeded in formalizing his grief in his poetry, but he could not restrain his sorrow over the death of his three-year-old Lottie. Few knowing of the circumstances would wish to hold him accountable for the sentimentality of the six or seven verses on Lottie included among the poems in the McGill Collection. Here, for example, is a stanza from one of them:

> Wake, my little maiden,
>   Wake, and bring me gleams,
> With bright fancies laden,
>   From the land of dreams;
> To the far eternal,
>   To the heights divine,
> To the great supernal,
>   Lead me, Lottie mine.

The birth (at Kingston) of another daughter, Florence, on August 17, 1868, only four months after Charlotte Mary's death, may have brought some consolation.[11]

In spite of the meagerness of Sangster's initial civil service salary, his financial situation was considerably improved over what it had been in Kingston. Some years after his death, his literary friend John Reade (1837–1919), of Montreal, in speaking of Sangster as a contributor to John Lovell's *Literary Garland*, put an anecdote on record which illustrates this. "Mr. Lovell," wrote Reade, "afterwards printed *Hesperus and Other Poems* for Mr. Sangster. Poets are rarely rich and a balance remained unpaid which Mr. Lovell had entirely forgotten, when one day he received a remittance from Sangster for the full amount. The poet had been appointed to a Post Office Department clerkship at Ottawa, and one of his first thoughts on accession to good fortune was to pay the printer."[12] What further proof could we ask of Sangster's honesty and integrity? Or, of the fact that he published *Hesperus* at a personal loss?

In October, 1868, a new poem of Sangster's appeared in *Stewart's Literary Quarterly Magazine*, which was published in Saint John, New Brunswick, by George Stewart, one of the most distinguished of nineteenth-century Canadian journalists. Another poem appeared in the January, 1869, issue; and to the April issue Sangster contributed a lengthy article on Charles Heavysege's *Saul*. Heavysege, whom E. H. Dewart ranked just below Sangster in his *Selections*, was an immigrant from England, a cabinet maker and newspaper reporter in Montreal, and one of the most unusual of poets. His massive closet dramas, Miltonic in ambition, are regarded today merely as literary curiosities, but in the nineteenth century his work reaped extravagant praise on both sides of the Atlantic. Longfellow, for example, described Heavysege as "the greatest dramatist since Shakespeare," and Emerson was only slightly less enthusiastic.[13] In his article, which is almost entirely synoptical and descriptive, Sangster simply echoes the critical opinion of the time. "First," he says, "on the list of the tuneful few who have contributed to our yet scanty stock of poetic literature, stands Mr. Charles Heavysege. . . . He stands, intellectually, a full head and shoulders above all others of the poetic race in the Dominion of Canada." Sangster's only regret is that Heavysege is not directing his talents toward specifically Canadian ends: "He is not at all Canadian in his choice of subjects. So far as that goes he might as well write and reside in Britain as here."

In summary, the 1860's were years of upheaval for Sangster. On the wings of *Hesperus* he soared from a position of promise to the pinnacle of an infant national literature. He acquired a new wife, two new daughters, and a new job in a new city. He lost a mother, a daughter, a fond city, and his accustomed health. The 1860's were also the crucible in which the Canadian nation was formed, and concealed in the mix was the germ of a poetic awakening that, within a generation, would all but obliterate the name of Charles Sangster from Canadian literary annals. The "poets of the sixties," as they are often called today, were all between eight and ten years of age by 1870.

CHAPTER 3

The Lost Years

I The 1870's

In essence, Sangster's problem in the early 1870's was that he had neither the health nor the leisure to continue his literary work in any more than a token way. His work load in the Post Office Department was heavy, and the routine was deadening. He regarded his job as the cause of both his poor health and his loss of poetic energy, but the problem may have gone deeper than that. He had, after all, known nothing other than routine drudgery all his working life, whether he was filling cartridges at Fort Henry, bookkeeping and proofreading at the *British Whig* office, or manipulating columns of figures at a desk in Ottawa. However, he believed that a less taxing job would see him restored to good health and enabled to pick up his literary work where he had left it off in the mid-1860's. It is evident from a letter which he wrote to David Gibson, of Kingston, in 1872 that he and his friends planned to get up a petition, probably for presentation to the prime minister, requesting that he be given more suitable employment. And this letter refers also to other of his personal woes. "My wife's health continues better," he writes, "but poor little Gertie [born 1870] is still ill. . . . At one time I feared that I would have to take her up and plant her in the sand at Waterloo. Now, however, she is slightly on the mend." To add to all this, the frequency with which he moved his family from one residence to another in Ottawa must have underlined his insecurity and frustration. He moved at least seven times during his term with the civil service, sometimes remaining at a given address for only a few months.[1]

There is a sequence of "Midnight Sonnets" in the McGill Collection which, as Desmond Pacey says, have all of Sangster's "melancholy introspectiveness at its ponderous worst." From a biographical standpoint, though, the sequence is more interesting. There are nine sonnets headed "Midnight" of the last day of each of the years from 1869 through 1877, and one other headed "1888–9 Perihelion." Patently, the "Midnight" sonnets are a log of Sangster's spiritual course through one of the most obscure decades of his life. The 1869 sonnet portrays a man still in the grasp of depression, loneliness, and bewilderment; contemplating the "strange paradox of life"; doubting his own powers of perception; and wondering if there is "one grain of sense" in his mundane existence. The plaint of the 1870 sonnet is similar: haunted by the "ghost of toil," he has had no time for his art, and no inspiration has come to him. He is a "galley slave," cursed and wronged by fate:

> Here lie my fancy-freighted argosies
> Becalmed, unvisited by breeze or gale,
> To rouse the sleeping waves or fill the sail
> And bring my merchandise across the seas.

A year later, he says that another year, "silent as destiny," has come and gone. Inertia alone has kept him going. Within his soul there is a deepening "gloaming" and clouds that "sternly lour." In the 1872 sonnet he likens himself to an eagle with its wings clipped, and the next year he writes disgustedly of his wasted life:

> O, frightful waste of life! O, woeful waste! ...
> No greater terror hath the gods devised
> Than the toil which makes men live and die in haste.

The 1874 sonnet is especially morbid. His thoughts, he says, are like dead trees which "lie strewn promiscuous on the ground":

> Through all my mind
> I seem to stumble over the dead past,
> As if there were no present.

It is hardly surprising to learn that Sangster suffered a nervous break-down in the early months of 1875. Some detail on this is provided in an unidentified editorial (presumably clipped from an Ottawa newspaper) in the McGill Collection. "Mr. Sangster," says the writer, "was performing his official labours under very great difficulties resulting in an almost complete loss of voice from nervous weakness." The writer refers to the doubts which were entertained in 1868 about Sangster's capacity to accept a Post Office appointment and states it to be his belief that Sangster "has never fulfilled" the duties of his clerical position. He goes on to speak of "a nervous attack which nearly prostrated him a few years since" and to make the following urgent plea: "Gentlemen of Mr. Sangster's literary ability should, in the interest of our infant Canadian literature, instead of being worked out physically, be reserved by light occupations for service to the world of letters. . . . Now is the time that appreciation should be manifested—not after the hand of death has pressed the life out of one of Canada's gifted sons."

The Post Office Department responded to Sangster's breakdown by appointing him private secretary to the deputy postmaster general, although he remained listed as a senior second-class clerk. He was pleased with the lighter duties of his new office, and his health rallied, but this was not the position he desired. We have only one letter from this period, and while it is a lengthy one, Sangster has taken such pains to avoid stating the facts, even to his friend David Gibson, that it is more tantalizing than informative. Here is part of the opening paragraph of this letter, which is dated November 24, 1875:

I have intended writing to you for some time past, but, as you very well know, didn't do it. Let that be my excuse. My brother wrote me that you had written out the certain paper that I sent him for a certain purpose, but just about that time I got transferred to the Secretary's Branch, and it became necessary to let the matter rest for the present. It will keep. The fact is I don't look on my present let down as a permanency, and many of my friends are determined to have me "let down" in some place where I can somewhat apply myself to my own lucubrations, which I cannot do here, although I am in a nice quiet place, with work which may be called trifling compared to my previous unending duties. These latter would have killed me in another year, and had I not kept pushing I would have been there still. A man who has been in danger of paralysis has to take care of himself. When the new Library is completed I will try and secure a quiet corner there where I can think for myself a little. My mind being easy, the rest I can do at home if I have fair play. Taking it all in all I have fought it through very well.

By "let down," he seems to mean "position" rather than "disappointment." He was not disappointed, but he had his eye on another position. It was not the postmastership at Kingston which he thought he should have, because he says jokingly: "If you give me the Postmastership when you superannuate that other harmless little man, Mr. Deacon, I will pull up stakes. There is nothing like looking up, if you want to see the stars." There are hints in the letter that his "promotion" was secured through political influence. We do not know his politics (if any, in a partisan sense), but Sir John A. Macdonald's Conservative government was defeated in November, 1873, and Alexander Mackenzie's Liberals were in power when he received his "promotion." This was to his disadvantage, he thought, after Macdonald's government was returned. But speculation on the basis of so little evidence is futile. Sangster's letter leaves no doubt, at least, about the seriousness of his recent illness or about his determination to continue with his "lucubrations." "See what it is to be famous, my friend," he writes, in concluding his letter, "I find in Bibaud's Supplement to Travaux's History of Canada: 'The St. Lawrence and the Saguenay,' by Charles *Langton*! "

Like the letter to David Gibson, the 1875 sonnet proclaims that the enemy of illness has been faced and conquered: "Respite! as when a prisoner set free/Sees, the first time in many weary years,/God's sunrise." The respite was short-lived. Sangster found that his lost muse did not return as his living and working conditions improved. The following lines are from the 1877 sonnet:

> My soul goes forth and searches through the dark
> To find a passage for the weary bark
> That I would pilot to the light beyond:
> But like the dove comes back my weary spark.

This is the last in the unbroken run of New Year's Eve sonnets.

Between 1870 and 1878, Sangster published sixteen poems in the leading Canadian journals—*Stewart's Quarterly*, *Canadian Monthly and National Review*, and *Belford's Monthly Magazine*. Though the claim made by most commentators that he abandoned his literary career entirely following the publication of *Hesperus* in 1860 is untrue, there is much more of failure than of success in the story of the last thirty years of his life. At the end of the 1870's, his artistic hopes were dormant—but not dead. Domestically, the decade closed well. His salary was raised to thirteen hundred dollars annually in 1879, and about the same time a son was born. The family, living at the time at 279 Maria Street, Ottawa, was then composed of Charles Sangster, 57; his wife, Henrietta, 36; Florence, 11; Gertrude, 9; and Roderick, an infant.[2]

II *Superannuation*

In the 1880's, the terms of superannuation from the public service were determined in each case by the Privy Council, and there was a certain amount of arbitrariness in the Privy Council's decisions. At least, this was Sangster's belief, and he took considerable pains, as we shall see, to present a strong case. His hope was that, in addition to the eighteen years (by 1886) served in Ottawa, he would be credited with the years he spent in the Ordnance Department in Kingston in the 1830's and 1840's. He explained his situation in his letter of February 1, 1883, to David Gibson:

If I could get John A. [Macdonald] & Company to do that for me which they have done for others (that is to allow me my ten years Imperial service) I would willingly go at once, but there might be great risk in asking seriously to be put on the retired list. My 15 years service which I will complete in May next; the ten years which they are permitted to add in all cases; and the 10 years Imperial service, would add up to 35 years, which would mean $980 dollars a year. . . . If I could get $900 (as Jenkins recently did—what did that numscull ever to for his country?) I would willingly drop the difference—$500 [less than his salary]—and make the government a present of that sum. I have been seriously thinking to try and induce George Fitzpatrick to aid in carrying the thing through for me, and he will be in a position to help from his position as Speaker, which I am glad to hear, as will all his Kingston friends, he is to have at the ensuing session. Still I fear the risk less they should drop me a peg or two lower if the case came up before the Council. The great difficulty would be the allowing of the Imperial 10 years, which I know of their having allowed in one case at least. . . . The only thing they have against me is the fact of [Liberal Prime Minister Alexander] Mackenzie having done a good thing for me. If I were a Frenchman, and [Alexander] Campbell ditto, seeing that he brought me here, he would do the handsome thing—for the French members never desert their nominees.

Sangster refrained from applying for his pension in 1883 because of the risk of being awarded an inadequate one, though he was seemingly pre-occupied by the question of retirement during the early 1880's. Little else is known of his activities during this period. In 1882, he was among the eighty charter members of the Royal Society of Canada, which was formed at the suggestion of the Marquis of Lorne, then governor general, to promote the development of science and literature. Sangster's literary friends Evan MacColl, William Kirby, John Reade, and George Stewart were also charter members of the society, as were such other distinguished Canadians as George M. Dawson, Sir Sanford Fleming, Louis H. Fréchette, Sir William Osler, Goldwin Smith, and Sir Daniel Wilson.

Sangster's second wife was living with him in 1883, but it is evident from his letters that she was not living with him in 1886. She predeceased him, and it is probable that she died between 1883 and 1886. If not, she separated from him at this time. Her death, or departure, may have contributed to the serious breakdown which he experienced in October, 1885. In any case, this breakdown convinced him that he must retire from the civil service, as he explains in the following letter to George Stewart:

OTTAWA
1st Feby 1886

MY DEAR MR. STEWART,

Will you excuse me for troubling you in regard to a little matter which may not be a small matter to me should I fail of success. I am compelled, chiefly from the condition of my nervous system, to ask for my superannuation this month, and before the House meets. When I was away last October on sick leave for a few weeks, suffering from nervous prostration, fever of brain, and weakness of the knees, so that I staggered as I walked, I mentally vowed that I would not run the risk of remaining in the P.O.D. another year. The condition I was in at that time was a warning to me, and gave me a scare which I must profit by.

I have only 18 years service, which is nothing, but I have a claim of 10 years in the Ordnance Department at Kingston from 1838 to 1849 (Imperial Service) which they should allow. They should allow it to count in my case as well as that of others. My intention was to ask you if you had a political friend (or more) who had influence with any members of the Privy Council, and whom you could inform of the fact that my application will likely come before the Council this month, and asking a good word from them for me if they can square it with their consciences.

It is harder now than formerly to get any time added to one's service. Were I a politician I would stand a better chance, but my claim is simply a literary one and not much at that. Still, I fancy I may have some claim on the country on that score, and think that they should consider my case favorably while they are about it, and grant me, as they have granted others, a fair allowance—many of them having chiefly their big salaries to recommend them. [Henry J.] Morgan, [keeper of the public records in the department of the secretary of state] will see Mr. [J. A.] Chapleau, [secretary of state], and I will do my best with my friends here and elsewhere, and there is no time to lose.

If you can serve me in this emergency through any of the political friends of the government, you will be conferring on me a great favor—lose or win. Someone having a good claim on Sir John [A. Macdonald] that he can use with certainty. I can point out no one myself, but I have written to [James] Lemoine [a well-connected Quebec writer] as well who may take a hand and who I suppose knows the ropes. I have literary work to do—a new edition and a volume brought here 18 years ago, and they ought to help me with that I am entitled, in addition to 6 months sick leave which I should get, and that would help to set me up. I am not fit for my literary work now, but had I a fair rest, and restored health, which let us hope for, I find there is a chance yet for my making up for lost time. My life here has been one of close application to the desk, and I should be glad to get that rest which I failed to get last year.

Not a word in your paper, please; it might spoil all, however good the intention.

Yours truly,

CHAS. SANGSTER.

George Stewart, who was editing a Quebec City newspaper at this time, received Sangster's letter on February 2, and forwarded it immediately to his friend Sir Adolphe Caron, minister of militia.

Sangster made formal application for a pension in February, 1886, and hoped for prompt action on it. Instead, he was given the six months' sick leave to which he was entitled—beginning March 1—and the decision was postponed until the expiration of the leave. It proved to be a period of anxiety and apprehension, because he was not sure that his allowance would be large enough to support him and his family. In a letter to William Kirby, dated April 20, 1886, he said: "They will not act on my application until my leave is expired. *Then*! —it depends a good deal on what I can wring from them, with that Lion, the Treasury Board, in my path. Were I a politician (on the right side) I could dictate terms, but I am nobody in particular and I must take pot luck. . . . They may put me off with half my salary—$700. I don't expect them to do anything handsome, so that I would have to watch the $ & ¢'s pretty close." He was hoping, as he had mentioned to David Gibson three years previously, to settle in Niagara after his release, and he was asking Kirby on this occasion about housing prospects there. Living with him at this time were his daughters, Florence and Gertrude, sixteen and seventeen years of age, and his son, Roderick, age six.

In May, 1886, he resigned from the Royal Society of Canada on the grounds that his nervous condition would not permit of his attending the meetings. He described the state of his health as follows to Kirby in a letter dated April 30, 1886:

My enforced holiday is doing me much good, and I feel a good deal stronger. A fever of brain with which I came back to work last October, and which came to the surface again this spring, is considerably relieved, and the only botheration remaining is that my knees have a little disposition to cave in and try to trip me up now and then, but I am much stronger in body, and quiet in mind, and keep a good deal in the open air, with just enough exercise to do me good without tiring me. . . .

I can't trust myself to read much just now and will endeavour to get all the rest of brain that I can before I settle down to the rough and tumble of whatever may turn up. Heretofore it has been all plain sailing, and the new life will be really new to me.

Upon his departure from Ottawa, Sangster did not establish himself for any length of time in Niagara, but he would seem to have spent the summer there. Lorne Pierce writes in his biography of Kirby: "Returning to Niagara, June 4 [1886] he [William Kirby] was delighted to have a visit from Charles Sangster. It was thirty years since the founder of the native choir of nature poets had published his first collection, and almost twenty-five since his last book had appeared. He had expected little, and life had given him less. It is hard to understand why so charming a man and so noble a poet should have lacked bread."

When the decision on the superannuation application was finally taken in September, 1886, it was (according to John Reade) Honorable Thomas White, minister of the interior, and a former journalist and publisher, who did most to secure Sangster a "fair" pension. However, the poet was far from pleased. In a letter to W. D. Lighthall, dated November 15, 1888, he said:

In superannuating me they gave me just enough to squeeze through on, many a political punk getting ahead of me by several hundred dollars—so much so that between you and I and the echoes, certain friends here threaten to compel Sir John [A. Macdonald] to make up the difference. . . .

When they get a man into the Civil Service, their first duty is to crush him flat, and if he is a fool of a poet, or dares to think of any nonsense of that kind, draw him through a knot of a gimlet hole a few times, pile on the agony of toil, toil until his nerves are flattened out, all the rebound knocked out of him, and then—superannuate him on what he can squeeze out of them through friends or enemies, and tell him he should be thankful for small favours of the most microscopic pattern.

It was as an embittered, sick, and impoverished man that Sangster returned to his native Kingston in September, 1886, after an absence of more than eighteen years.

III   *The Last Years*

The principal source of material on Sangster's last years is the series of fifteen letters in the McGill Collection which the poet wrote to W. D. Lighthall of Montreal between 1888 and 1893. The correspondence began on July 2, 1888, when Lighthall wrote to Sangster asking him where he might obtain copies of his books, as Lighthall wished to include some of Sangster's poems in his anthology, *Songs of the Great Dominion*. "There is nothing more pathetic in all our literary history," says Desmond Pacey, "than these last letters of Sangster's, in which he records the terrible effort with which he is revising and arranging his poetry."

In a letter to Lighthall dated July 8, 1888, Sangster says:

I have written comparatively nothing for the past twenty years—I might say positively nothing. I came back to this my native city in September,

1886, having been compelled to leave the Post Office Department at Ottawa on a superannuation allowance owing to the breaking down of my nervous system after eighteen years of steady desk work. I took the MS of a thin volume on my leaving here at the request of the Hon. (now Sir) A. Campbell down to Ottawa, put it aside when I assumed my labour at the desk, and left it laid on the shelf for those eighteen years, but found no time either to publish, or to add anything to it for all that time, so steady were my duties, and so much did they unfit me for any, even the slightest, literary endeavour.

> The King Of France, with twice ten thousand men
> Marched up the hill, and then marched down again!

And that was the case with my MSS. I took them to Ottawa— I brought them back to Kingston.

Two years elapsed in Kingston before he was able to set about his work again and belatedly prepare his unpublished poems for publication. His July 8, 1888 letter to Lighthall continues: "Since coming back I have gained considerably in health—50% or thereabouts, but it is only now that I feel that I dare use my brain, to set my papers in order, which I am now doing slowly to the best of my ability."

While Sangster was engaged in keeping house at Kingston, working on his manuscripts, and trying to fight off rheumatism and nervous illness, some of his friends were using their influence to have Queen's University confer an honorary degree upon him. In his letters, Sangster speaks of the "Queen's College affair" and of "that mysterious degree," but he is loath to consider accepting any proposal which might be made. "It would be more in Evan MacColl's line than in mine," he wrote to Lighthall, on February 13, 1889; "MacColl likes that sort of thing—I don't." He had his way. Queen's University has no record of his ever having been proposed as a candidate for an honorary degree.

Sangster soon came to regard Lighthall as his literary executor, a role which Lighthall gracefully accepted, although he must have appreciated the futility of Sangster's latter-day struggle to put his manuscripts in order for publication. But Lighthall was obviously moved by the plight of the aging poet and became the sort of sympathetic literary confidant which Sangster should have had all of his life. It was Lighthall, it would seem, to whom the thought of a Queen's College honor had first occurred. When Sangster shied away from that, Lighthall made him an honorary member of the Society of Canadian Literature of Montreal, a society which he himself had formed.

In the spring of 1891 Sangster was again taken with the idea of moving to Niagara. He wrote to Kirby on March 30:

DEAR MR. KIRBY,

One of my daughters will probably be leaving me shortly, and I still have a hankering after your locality. I know no commission agent to write to, besides these people cannot always be depended upon, so I fall back upon someone I do know and can depend upon.

Are there any houses to rent there? When I was at Niagara Town there were none, nor any signs of there being any to rent, as no new ones were going up. I would be much obliged could you inform me at your earliest leisure. There are only three of us, and should my little boy of twelve happen to stay behind for the present, only two.

House or cottage, with a probability of changing for a cottage soon in the case of a house. Were the boats running I could easily run up, but I dread the long trip by rail, and could not risk it—besides the expense is so great. . . .

Business before pleasure. My brain is well nigh worn out keeping house, and I think that if there is a chance for me, that the change might do me good. Just now I can neither read, nor write, nor think. Your atmosphere might restore all this, or partially so, and my work is not finished. Many things have conspired to keep me back, but it seems to me that the grand view of the lake alone would go a long way towards easing me mentally.

I am sorry to trouble you but "needs must when the devil drives," to quote an old proverb. Still, I don't believe in a personal old devil, and I hope very few of my personal friends do. Kind regards to Mrs. Kirby.

> Yours fraternally,
> CHARLES SANGSTER.

Kirby was successful in finding a cottage on this occasion, and Sangster embarked for Niagara about the first of May.

By July, 1891, Sangster's health had reached a perilous new low, and he wrote as follows to Lighthall:

NIAGARA, ONT., July 4, 1891

DEAR MR. LIGHTHALL:

Pending the possibility of anything serious happening in these Perihelion times, I take the liberty of sending the accompanying notes for safe-keeping by your society or yourself, as you shall please to decide. My nerves are so shaky at times and I am liable to spells of dizziness that I think it is best to take this precaution in advance. I will send the remainder of the MSS as it is completed, if you and the rest of my literary friends have no objection. More anon when I hear from you. The above is my present address.

> Yours sincerely,
> CHARLES SANGSTER.

By September, 1891, he had mailed almost all of his unpublished poetry to Lighthall but, to the end of his life, he continued to send him brief letters about the manuscripts. In 1892, he moved back to Ottawa and would seem to have resided there—at 412 Lewis Street—until the spring of 1893, when he took sufficient time off from illness to visit Cleveland, Ohio, before returning to live in Kingston. It must be to the summer of 1893 that Wallace H. Robb returns us with the following reminiscence:

In Pittsburgh Township, south edge, Lot D in the 1878 Atlas, is the Sibbitt home, an old limestone manor-house still occupied by my neighbours, Ed and Ross Sibbitt. In 1950, their eldest brother, the late Ex-Reeve John Sibbitt, gave me his recollections of Sangster, who boarded for a while one summer with their widowed mother. From my notes, let me reconstruct our conversation: Remember Charlie Sangster? Yes, indeed, very clearly—he was an odd duck. It was between 1890 and 1893. Sangster was very old—looked it, with long, flowing hair and beard. He used to wander alone on the shore and through all the nearby countryside. . . .

He had an odd habit of never coming back from a ramble empty-handed; nearly always a great armful of dry sticks from the woods. And he would sit on the woodpile, or anything, by the back door, for long periods, quietly thinking, watching who knows what! Birds, men at haying, boats on the river—not seeming to see anything. Sometimes he would sit with mother in the kitchen, silent—a queer bird. He seemed to believe in some kind of spirits: he sometimes complained in the morning that they had kept him awake. Charlie Sangster was a nice, old fellow; he seemed weary and downhearted—a sad and lonely old man with soft, darkish eyes and patriarchal beard like Father Time. We liked him, but couldn't understand him.

The end was at hand.

IV *Death and After Years*

Charles Sangster died in Kingston on December 9, 1893, at the home of his nephew, William Sangster, 398 Barrie Street. His body was taken for burial to Cataraqui Cemetery, Kingston, where his grave can still be seen, marked by a small monument with the simple type of inscription he would have preferred: "Charles Sangster POET."

The Toronto *Globe* (December 11) offered a brief editorial:

Thirty-three years have elapsed since the publication of Sangster's *Hesperus* and thirty-seven since *The St. Lawrence and the Saguenay* appeared. They won him more than a Canadian reputation, and were favorably reviewed by such men as Bayard Taylor and Oliver Wendell Holmes. In recent years Mr. Sangster has written very little, but he has had the pleasure of seeing his works firmly established as Canadian Classics. No collection of Canadian verse has been considered as complete without some of his fine descriptions of Canadian scenery and history.

In the *Week* (February 2, 1894), Sangster's old friend and admirer, Reverend E. H. Dewart, wrote:

Charles Sangster, the poet, is dead. . . . It is not too much to say that among all the life-histories of English bards who battled with unpropitious fortune, poverty, and neglect, there is scarcely one who has had a rougher or steeper path to climb, or faced unfriendly fate with a braver heart than he. . . .

He has for years past kept so much in the shades of retirement that many of the younger generation of readers will ask, who is Charles Sangster? And yet he long stood as our most representative Canadian poet.

Can it be said that a poet who received the approbation which the reviewers gave to both of Sangster's volumes was neglected or unappreciated? Sangster was looking not only to the critics and reviewers. Sales of both volumes were discouragingly poor. Writing in 1896, Dewart stated that "instead of being a source of profit, the proceeds of the sales did not pay the cost of publication. There must be a supply of *Hesperus* lying unsold somewhere to this day." The true barometer of public recognition to Sangster's mind was appointment to an honorary position in the public service, the sinecure being the nineteenth-century mode of using public funds to support artists and others considered to be promoting the national interest through nonremunerative activity. Sangster's appointment to the Post Office Department came too late, and as we have seen it was not a sinecure which he received, but a position of routine drudgery, which snuffed out any remaining spirit which he may have had. He came to feel increasingly that little or no genuine appreciation of his achievement existed in Canada, and, of course, he was quite right. E. K. Brown put it only slightly differently. "Sangster received a great deal of encouragement," said Brown, "but he did not have around him that atmosphere of eager sympathy with poetry that is the most precious kind of encouragement, without which all other encouragement is a little artificial and in the end insufficient."[3]

If Sangster was not appreciated during his lifetime, at least he was treated with respect by his literary contemporaries—Dewart, Stewart, Kirby, Lighthall, and Reade—to mention those who displayed particular interest and concern. The disrespect shown his memory following his death does not reflect favorably upon Canadians. Lighthall deposited the Sangster manuscripts at McGill (for which we may be thankful), and there they lay—"lost," in effect, for more than fifty years. Arthur Bourinot, whose 1946 essay on Sangster was a welcome break in a long critical silence, tried to locate the manuscripts in the 1940's but was informed, he said, by McGill that the manuscripts were not there. Desmond Pacey was successful, however, in locating them at McGill in 1957, while he was preparing his *Ten Canadian Poets*. The dearth of biographical material has been both described and demonstrated. No new biographical information was published between 1896 (Dewart) and 1958 (Pacey). All critical and biographical commentary published during this period was second-hand and, with all of the repetition and quotations from the poetry which it contained, would fill no more than twenty-five pages.

No memorial or monument of any sort was erected until 1964. Pacey recommended in 1958 that the house in which Sangster died in Kingston be marked by the Historic Sites and Monuments Board or by some other agency. Finally, the Ontario Archeological and Historic Sites Board, on the recommendation of the Kingston Historical Society, placed a historic marker in the Cricket Field in Kingston. The address at the unveiling of this marker, on September 12, 1964, was delivered by H. Pearson Gundy of Queen's University, a member of the Kingston Historical Society. It might be well to conclude this chapter with a few brief passages from Mr. Gundy's address on that occasion:

Charles Sangster, to whom we pay belated honour this afternoon, might well qualify as our most neglected national poet. . . .
We can, perhaps, take some small comfort in the fact that Charles Sangster was never completely forgotten in the city of his birth, for here in Kingston, his grand-niece, Miss Marion Sangster, in her own quiet way, has kept his memory green. Another member of our Historical Society, Miss Jessie Polson, can remember as a small girl seeing Sangster in the company of his friend William Sawyer, Kingston artist, portrait-painter, and the grandfather of another of our members, Colonel W. R. Sawyer of the Royal Military College. . . .
Sangster was not a faultless poet, for such a poet has yet to be born. But that his poetic faults should have eclipsed and obscured his genuine merit is an undeserved fate, the aftermath of time and neglect. Let us hope, then, that this marker which we dedicate this afternoon will in some measure help to re-establish the worth of Charles Sangster.[4]

Sangster would probably not have asked for more. "Fame is dross to me," he said, "I write because I believe it to be a duty; and, succeed or fail, what little light I have shall not be hidden under a bushel." There is no reason to question this altruism. Sangster's infirmities were many, but that last infirmity of noble minds was near the bottom of the list.

CHAPTER 4

The St. Lawrence and the Saguenay

I *The Journey in the Title Poem*

The title poem in *The St. Lawrence and the Saguenay* is Sangster's most ambitious poem; it is the obvious introduction to his work because it provides evidence of most of his interests and attitudes and of most of his strengths and weaknesses as a poet. It is closely modeled on *Childe Harold's Pilgrimage* both in concept and in execution. Byron cast descriptions of the travels and reflections of a pilgrim in Europe into Spenserian stanzas. Sangster employs the same stanza to capture the impressions of a voyager from Lake Ontario, down the Saint Lawrence, and up the Saguenay as far as Port Alfred. He writes in the first person. The geographical signposts provide the unifying thread, but his impressions are not exclusively, or even primarily, pictorial impressions of scenes and places along the route. Rather, again in the manner of Byron, he recalls history and legend and reflects upon a wide range of other subjects.

Sangster is accompanied on his imaginary journey by an ethereal female companion, to whom the two opening stanzas are devoted. She is the source of his poetic inspiration, and in the following stanza he bids her conduct his spirit's course:

> Maiden! from whose large intellectual eyes,
> My soul first drank love's immortality,
> Plume my weak spirit for its chosen skies,
> 'T would falter in its mission without thee.
> Conduct its flight; and if its musings be
> Oft'ner of earth than heaven, bear awhile
> With what is native to mortality:
> It dare not err exulting in thy smile:
> Look on it with thine eyes, and keep it free from guile. [II]

Before discussing the literary characteristics of the poem, let us trace the route of the four-hundred-mile journey from Sangster's home city of Kingston to Ha Ha Bay in the heartland of the Saguenay. The "bark leaps love-fraught from the land" into the lake (which is calmed by echoes from "The Lotus Eaters") and glides to the Thousand Islands:

> Isle after isle
> Is passed, as we glide tortuously through
> The opening vistas, that uprise and smile
> Upon us from the ever-changing view.
> Here nature, lavish of her wealth, did strew
> Her flocks of panting islets on the breast
> Of the admiring River. . . . [IV]

The Thousand Islands, famed for their beauty far beyond the ravings of pilgriming romantics, furnish the inspiration for more than twenty stanzas as well as for the beautiful "Lyric to the Isles." Reflections on nature, love, art, and other subjects come readily to the poet among these magical islands, which have been part of his environment since childhood.

A thunderstorm breaks, occasioning a lyrical "Hymn to the Lightning" and thoughts on the music of nature and poetry. Twilight falls, bringing a "Twilight Hymn," and with a full-orbed moon irradiating the night sky, the fantasy craft moves through the swift-flowing waters of the Saint Lawrence River:

> Swift through the sinuous path our vessel glides,
> Now hidden by the massive promontories,
> Anon the bubbling silver from its sides
> Spurning, like a wild bird, whose home is on the tides. [XXXI]

The treacherous Saint Lawrence rapids are run in a single stanza:

> The startled Galloppes shout as we draw nigh,
> The Sault, delighted, hails our reckless bark,
> The graceful Cedars murmurs joyously,
> The vexed Cascades threaten our little ark,
> That sweeps, love-freighted, to its distant mark.
> Again the troubled deep heaps surge on surge,
> And howling billows sweep the waters dark. [XXXVI]

The Lachine rapids behind, Mount Royal rises into view above the city of Montreal, where the Indian village of Hochelaga once stood. As Montreal's Saint Helen's Island is reached, the Tennysonian echoes are muted, and strains from Coleridge and Milton can be heard playing in the background:

> St. Helenes next, a fair, enchanted ground,
> A stately Isle in glowing foliage dressed,
> Laved by the dark St. Lawrence all around,
> Giving a grace to its enamored breast,
> As pleasing to the eye as Hochelaga's crest. [XXXVIII]

Apart from the recollection of a childhood romance with a Montreal lass, the city calls forth few impressions from the poet. A "Canzonet" to summer is interposed, and the journey is resumed.

The Saint Lawrence between Montreal and Quebec City, a distance of some one hundred and fifty miles, flows through a region as rich in history and color as any in Canada, but in three stanzas we are swept from Montreal to Cap Santé:

> And here,
> Varennes, like a fair Eden purged from guile,
> Sits smiling on the night. . . .[XLV]

> Swift through the Richilieu! Past the white sands
> That spangle fair Batiscan's pleasant shore
> We glide. . . . [XLVI]

> That is St. Pierre,
> Where the tall poplars—which the night bedims
> Lift their sharp outlines through the solemn air.
> Past these white cottages to L'Avenir,
> Another site of beauty. Lovlier yet,
> The Plateau, slumbering in foliage there;
> And gay Cap Sainte, like a Wild Love, beset
> With wooers, bringing gems to deck her coronet. [XLVII]

(It will have been noticed that some of the place names have been misspelled—in either language—and since L'Avenir is in Drummond County, some seventy miles from the Saint Lawrence, we can assume, perhaps, that Sangster had the name confused with Lotbiniere.)

A song fills the night air, and we hear the lyric to the "Whippoorwill" before Quebec City comes into view, and Sangster's thoughts go back to the Battle of the Plains of Abraham:

> Quebec! how regally it crowns the height,
> Like a tanned giant upon a solid throne!
> Unmindful of the sanguinary fight,
> The roar of cannon mingling with the moan

> Of mutilated soldiers years agone,
> That gave the place a glory and a name
> Among the nations. . . . [L]

There is a pause at Quebec City to ponder its romantic history and view the natural beauty of its surroundings. The craft moves along the shore of Quebec and Montmorency counties, where the poet gets a favorable impression of the habitants:

> A courteous, gentle race, as ever blent
> Religion with Simplicity. The cheer
> That greets the stranger who may wander here
> Glows with the zeal of hospitality. [LVI]

Perhaps no sentimental visitor to the Quebec City area could avoid Ile-d'Orléans, however disembodied he might be, or however intent upon escaping from geography. On the shores of the island, says Sangster, "glancing spires . . . silver in the moon" and "sparkling villages" brood. A "Parting Song" rises as the craft moves onward down the river.

The little island of Ile-aux-Coudres and Baie Saint Paul opposite it on the north side of the river present a tranquil scene:

> This isle might guard the entrance to a sphere
> Of heavenly tranquility! The mind
> Puts off its weight of cares, for Beauty here
> Sits like a wondrous deity enshrined
> Among the hills. Oh, God! but Thou art kind!
> St. Paul's delightful Bay, fit mirror for
> The stars, glows like a vision which the wind
> Wafts by some Angel standing on the shore. [LXV]

Les Eboulements (although its name is misspelled) is tenderly pictured:

> Eboullemens sleeps serenely in the arms
> Of the Maternal hill, upon whose breast
> It lies. . . . [LXVIII]

The "granite sternness" of La Malbaie (Murray Bay) is left behind, the sun rises to a "Paen to the Dawn," and suddenly the craft is being tossed about by the "black and frowning waters of the Saguenay."

The St. Lawrence and the Saguenay

In contrast with the valley of the Saint Lawrence, the Saguenay is a forbidding land of "iron hills" and "dwarfish evergreens":

> Pile on pile
> The granite masses rise to left and right:
> Bold stately bluffs that never wear a smile;
> Where vegetation fails to reconcile
> The parched shubbery and stunted trees
> To the stern mercies of the flinty soil. [LXXXIX]

A lyric entitled "Vanished Hopes" expresses the mood induced by the Saguenay.

Finally, Ha Ha Bay, a seeming oasis of life, is reached:

> A stately ship lies anchored in the bay:
> Like an Oasis to the Desert child,
> It speaks of life. . . . [XCIII]

The poet's spirit rises in a "Song" of hope, and the journey ends at nearby Trinity Rock.

II *Meaning in the Title Poem*

The narrative in "The St. Lawrence and the Saguenay" is not prominent enough to give the poem coherence. It was Sangster's intention that the river journey symbolize his spirit's search for the fount of poetic inspiration, and had he been successful in developing the second level of meaning the over-all result would have been more satisfying. However, he so obscured his design that no commentator on the poem has mentioned the symbolic level of meaning, in spite of the fact that its recognition is vital to a comprehension of the six concluding stanzas of the poem and to an understanding of the role of the spiritlike companion on the voyage. Throughout the poem, Sangster broods over the question of poetic inspiration. The goal of the journey is Trinity Rock in the Saguenay country, and when we examine the lines describing the achievement of that goal, it becomes evident not only that, symbolically, the journey has been a quest for the true source of poetic inspiration but also that the poet is receiving his call, in the manner of the Prophets of the Old Testament, to be a witness of nature.

At the Rock (called the "Monarch of the Bluff"), nature, through her sun's eye, is looking down "in mild unutterable grace," when suddenly her "light," or inspiration, strikes the poet, and at the same time, the truth being imparted to him is presented pictorially in a "vision" of the "Monarch of the Bluff":

> Strong eager thoughts come crowding to my eyes. . . .
> As in stern grandeur, looming up the skies,
> This Monarch of the Bluff, with kingly grace
> Stands firmly. . . . [CII]

This experience parallels the experiences of Isaiah, Jeremiah, and Amos, when they were called to be prophets of God.[1] And just as they were all dumbfounded by the call to serve God, so is the poet literally struck dumb by the call to serve nature: "My lips are mute. I cannot speak the thought/That, like a bubble in the placid sea/Bursts ere it tells the tale with which 'tis fraught" [CIII]. Trinity Rock, which represents nature in the vision, weeps for joy at the poet's acceptance of the call: "Like tears of gladness o'er a giant's face/The streams leap perpendicularly down/The polished sides of the steep precipice" [CIV].

The poet's spiritual search is over; he has become a poet of nature. It is only at this point that we realize who the companion of his journey has been. That maiden from whom his "soul first drank love's immortality" was the *only one*, he said, in the first line of the poem, to whom his hopes were clinging. She was not the "spirit of nature," but the "spirit of love," his original source of poetic inspiration. She led him to nature, but now that he has been called to be a nature poet, he must abandon her in favor of the higher inspiration: "The goal is won,/Here, by this Rock, 't is doomed that we must part/And part forever . . ." [CV]. And finally he embraces the spirit of nature enthusiastically:

> All, all is thine love now: Each thought and hope
> In the long future must be shared with thee.
> Lean on my bosom; let my strong heart ope
> Its fount of love, that the wild ecstacy
> That quickens every pulse, and makes me free
> As a God wishes, may serenely move
> Thy inmost being with the mystery
> Of the new life that has just dawned. [CX]

Why does Sangster fail so dismally to project his meaning? First, the poem is highly undisciplined. Instead of being presented in any logical order, ideas and impressions have been thrown together randomly. Even the crucial Trinity Rock scene itself has the flavor of an eleventh hour attempt to wrest some sort of significance from a welter of confusion. The second reason for his failure to make his point is even more important and more ominous for his career as a poet than the first. It is simply that his vocabulary for dealing with abstract concepts is both limited and woolly. "Love," "Nature," "Truth," "Virtue," "Beauty," "Intellect," "Genius," and the nest of similar terms in which he so frequently takes refuge are employed with such slovenliness that they lose their separate identities and become little more than different ways of spelling the Great Abstraction. "Love" was his first inspiration, but love of what? There is no assurance that he means sexual love; he may mean love of art or love of beauty or love of love. There is no "love story" in "The St. Lawrence and the Saguenay," in any but the most esoteric sense of the term; yet it is usually stated that there is a love story, since Sangster employs the term "love" so frequently and assigns female attributes helter-skelter to the airiest of abstractions.

III *Themes in the Title Poem*

Since the search for a central core of meaning in the poem yields little, we must be content to examine its more obvious characteristics. Nature is foremost among the subjects treated in the poem. It was Sangster's interest in nature rather than his skill as poet or philosopher which led one reviewer to describe him as "the Wordsworth of Canada." Like Wordsworth, he is not content only to describe nature; he also desires to be nature's interpreter. He joys in communion with the natural world:

> A wild joy fills my overburdened brain.
> My ears drink music from each thunder peal.
> I glory in the lightnings and the rain.
> There is no joy like this! With thee to feel
> And share each impulse. . . .   [XVIII]

He sees God's hand behind nature:

> Over the darkening waters! On through scenes
> Whose unimaginable wildness fills
> The mind with joy insatiate, and weans
> The soul from earth, to Him whose presence thrills
> All Beauty as all Truth. . . . [LXXXII]

Sometimes, as in the "Hymn to Lightning," his utterances are pantheistic, but he always proclaims God's transcendence:

Thy Voice is in the thunder cloud,
Thy Presence in the lightning's fire—
Breathings of an Almighty Ire,
   That wraps the heavens in a shroud

Of blinding light, before whose heat
The granite mountains melt away,
And finite man falls down to pray
   For mercy at his Maker's feet.

He would be nature's interpreter, but time and again (to his everlasting credit!) he proclaims his inadequacy:

My love is strong as yon enduring Rock!
Deep as the thoughtful waters at its feet! —
Oh! could my willing voice find words t' unlock
Its depths, and free the sleeping echoes, fleet
As the swift-footed chamois, they would greet
The far-surrounding hills with such a tale
Of passion as had never left its seat
Within the heart of man. . . . [CVIII]

His approach to nature in the poem is by no means original. His treatment of the subject is the product of a genuine sensitivity to the world around him and a fashionable Romantic pose. Had he shunned this kind of imitativeness, he would have written better poetry. When he tries to be profound, he becomes dull and often incomprehensible; when he contents himself with simple description, he is often interesting and colorful.

It is not really possible to separate Sangster's devotion to nature from his devotion to God, or his nature poetry from his religious poetry. "The St. Lawrence and the Saguenay" is infused with religious faith. There is no subtlety whatever in Sangster's religion, and he feels no compulsion to justify his faith. Reason has no place in religion, he thinks. "Deep thinking" is the cause of doubt, which only faith itself can dispel:

I knew a man whose prayerful soul was set
To a devotional music, like a psalm
Fresh from a Master-Artist's brain; and yet,
There came a time when his mind's starriest calm
Was quenched in Unbelief. Once, like a palm
He flourished, till deep thinking brought a doubt
Of a Hereafter, and the Great I AM!
Like a new light, Faith slowly came, and out
Of his dark world he strode, believing and devout. [LXXIII]

Most of his expressions of faith in the poem are just as unspeakably banal as this one is. Exceptions are a number of his hymns, in which his conventional piety and lyrical gift are combined to good effect. Here, for example, is the first stanza of "Twilight Hymn," the most successful of the interlude hymns in "The St. Lawrence and the Saguenay":

> God of the early Morning light!
>> Whose hand the Gates of Dawn unbars;
> God of the Evening and the Night!
>> Who guides the chariots of the stars:
> We thank thee for the air we breathe,
>> The waves that roll, the winds that rise,
> For all thy wondrous works beneath,
>> For all the glories of the skies.

Also inseparable often from the nature and religion themes is the theme of the poet's own inner state of being—his introspective, or "soul," poems. In "The St. Lawrence and the Saguenay," the always morose, sometimes morbid note of these poems is most nearly reached in the lyrical interlude entitled "Vanished Hopes":

> I've supped with depression and feasted with sorrow,
>> The hot tears of anguish have withered my heart;
> And now, death might strike down my last hope tomorrow,
>> Not one tear is left me to deaden his dart.

The theme of love is not prominent, as we have seen, in "The St. Lawrence and the Saguenay." The mystical companion on the voyage, even if she is considered to exist on the literal level, does not add love interest to the poem. That leaves only the sweetheart of his boyhood days, whom he recalls in the Montreal stanzas. He loved her, he says, with "deep passion," and his love has grown with time. He paints her as an ideal beauty with joyful blue eyes (unusual in Sangster, who preferred brown), a lovely face, and lovelier lips:

> There was a joyousness within her eyes,
> Like the sun's light illumining the blue
> Of heaven, making earth a paradise.
> Gladness, like a celestial spirit passing through
> The gates of morn, rose white-winged on the view,
> When e'er you looked upon her lovely face,
> Love sat upon her lips, and love's sweet dew
> Fell from them, leaving there a sunny trace,
> As if touched by angel's wings they caught angelic grace. [XLI]

National pride is implied in the poem by the emotion displayed for all things Canadian, from the thunderstorm to the whippoorwill, and from the Thousand Islands to Montmorency Falls. When his thoughts turn to historical events, his pride sometimes swells with patriotism. The sight of Cape Diamond at Quebec City quite naturally turns his thoughts back to 1759. The Cape, he says, has "no trivial trust" in guarding Wolfe's memory. Even if the cenotaph on the plain should be destroyed through rebellious "lust for spoilation" (prophetic words!), the Cape is a monument which will always stand. Although Wolfe is Sangster's hero supreme (as he was, and is, the hero of many other Canadians), he has almost equal admiration for Montcalm. He is pleased that the two heroes are honored together: "Wolfe and Montcalm! two nobler names ne'er graced/The page of history, or the hostile plain" [LI].

Sangster is moved not only by the great dramatic events of history but also by the romance of the past—by the voyageurs and above all by the North American Indians. As the craft glides down the Saint Lawrence under cover of night, he thinks of the voyageurs who once traveled the same route:

> Long years ago the early Voyageurs
> Gladdened these wilds with some romantic air:
> The moonlight, dancing on their dripping oars,
> Showed the slow batteaux passing by with care,
> Impelled by rustic crews. . . . [XIII]

At the Thousand Islands, he recalls the legend of an Indian girl whose father was a fugitive on one of the islands. Even on the "wildest midnight" the girl would "cross the tide" to minister to her father's needs. She is known as the Queen of the Isles, and she deserves to be remembered, the poet thinks, on page and canvas. In this poem, as in many others, he laments the passing of the noble Red Man with as much evident sincerity as Longfellow, his mentor on this subject, conveys.

Most of the themes of Sangster's poetry are touched upon in "The St. Lawrence and the Saguenay." The themes are developed in a variety of ways, of course, in his other poems, and the emphases do not remain the same, but these are the subjects in which he is interested.

IV Criticism of the Title Poem

As a prelude to discussing some of the artistic strengths and weaknesses displayed by Sangster in "The St. Lawrence and the Saguenay," most of the critical commentary which has been published on the poem during the past century is quoted below. How unusual it seems that essentially all of the criticism on the lengthiest single work of the principal Canadian poet of the pre-Confederation era can be printed on two or three pages and would not fill a page if the repetition were eliminated! The aim has been to quote the following statements in their entirety, omitting only quotations which the commentators used from the poem, and any irrelevancies:

It is a pleasant and tasteful depiction of the scenes and associations of our noble river, written in the same stanza as *Childe Harold*, and with some echo of its mode of thought, though lacking the force and pathos of its passionate utterances.[2] —Daniel Wilson (1858)

Rough, uncouth lines are to be found. . . . There is much to admire and appreciate.[3] —George Stewart (1869)

The chief poem portrays an imaginary voyage of the poet, and some fair but shadowy companion, down the St. Lawrence and up the Saguenay. It consists mainly of descriptive references to places and scenes along the shores of these mighty rivers, and such poetic musings as these scenes, or events of which they were the theatres, inspire. The Thousand Islands, Montreal, Quebec, and the bold scenery of the lone Saguenay, stir the soul of the patriotic bard, and call forth appropriate reflections. At intervals there is a burst of lyrical melody from the voyager, as if the measured movement of the more stately metre was too prosaic to fitly express the joyous admiration that thrilled him. Some of these are his best lyrics. The poem consists of one hundred and ten Spenserian stanzas.—E. H. Dewart (1896)

Glowingly he takes us, in "St. Lawrence and the Saguenay," down the grandeurs of that unrivalled tour—the great River, its rapids, cities, mountains, and "Isles of the Blest."[4] —W. D. Lighthall (1899)

The hundred and ten Spenserian stanzas of the leading poem form a kind of descriptive guidebook to the rivers mentioned in the title. On every page there is, as the *Athenaeum* remarked with great justice, "a feeling for the beauties of nature"; but there is also, as it added, "a general vagueness" that prevents adequate visualization. Though the phrasing is occasionally felicitous, the lines are marred by false rhymes and incongrous diction. The lyrics too lack spontaneity and grace.[5] —R. P. Baker (1920)

The title poem of the first volume is in the Spenserian stanza as employed by Byron and is also otherwise imitative. But it is distinctly Canadian in its lyrical interludes, in which there is a poetic *abandon* to the beauty and magic of Nature in Canada . . . expressing a *new* note, *the* Canadian note in Canadian poetry. It is, however, a *nature* note, not or hardly the *national*

[63]

note—clear and confident and strong.[6]—J. D. Logan and D. G. French (1924)

His handling of the Spenserian stanza is frequently faulty.[7]—Lorne Pierce (1927)

The chief poem in the first volume is a kind of sentimental journey, or Childe Harold's pilgrimage, in which the poet and some fair but imaginary companion sail down the great river and respond with appropriate emotions to the beauty and variety of the scenery or the sacredness of historical associations. The poem consists of a hundred and ten Spenserian stanzas and some lyrical interludes. The mingling of various influences—Byron and Scott particularly, and even (in one couplet at least) Pope's *Pastorals*—with Sangster's direct observations make these skilfully handled Spenserian stanzas interesting to the student of literature as well as the lover of pure poetry or to the sentimental traveller. The poem is episodic and not without some dull and inflated passages, but the description of the Thousand Islands is an elegant and successful piece of writing.—A. J. M. Smith (1943)

The chief poem in *The St. Lawrence and the Saguenay and Other Poems* is the one which gives the title to the book. It is a long work in the Spenserian stanza form, interspersed with lyrics, and is descriptive of a journey through the Thousand Islands, the St. Lawrence and the Saguenay Rivers. The work is uneven but contains some fine passages, particularly the opening stanzas and the "Lyric to the Isles." His nature descriptions are excellent and some of the lyrics sing themselves to the reader. Many of the stanzas, however, are marred by weak and faulty rhythm and by phraseology that is not particularly apt to the occasion. Some of the lines are memorable. . . . It would be interesting to see what changes the poet made in the poem in later life.[8]—Arthur S. Bourinot (1946)

The title poem is diffuse, vague, and ridiculously inflated in diction, but some of its images are bold and striking, and some of its descriptive passages are well-observed. . . . But it must be admitted that even most of the description is conventional, and as a narrative the poem is very weak. There is not sufficient variety in the scenes to hold the attention for the poem's full length, and the love story, which might have provided momentum, is so obscure that it merely tantalizes the reader. The passion is talked about rather than communicated. . . .—Desmond Pacey (1958)

In *The St. Lawrence and the Saguenay* (1856) he composed Spenserian stanzas with sedulous care; but like all imported mannerism, his treatment did not convey the reality of the local subject matter, and his sense of form was entirely mechanical. . . . There is no proof that the Spenserian

stanza cannot be used in Canada, or in the Himalayas for that matter . . .
but in Sangster the borrowing is still slavish and the form oddly archaic?
—Louis Dudek (1967)

Let us consider first the more general of the adverse remarks of the
commentators. Both Baker and Pacey say that the poem is "vague." We
have already been concerned with two of the reasons for this: the absence
of discipline and the perplexing manner in which abstract ideas are
expressed. There are other reasons as well. The very fact that Sangster
favors the abstract over the concrete and generality over particularity leads
to diffuseness. And the conventional wording and phrasing of most of the
poem paralyzes thought and emotion.

The commentators are agreed that the diction of the poem is "inflated"
or "incongruous." Indeed, Sangster's clime, oft'ner than not, is a bless'd
Eden where such sprites as the Genius of Love, the lightsome Dream of
Art, the Sun of Hope, and ev'n the desp'rate Demon Woe disport themselves in the soft verdure, 'neath umbrageous birchen trees, as from yonder
enchanted isles of stately evergreens and shepherd vales, Zephyrus wafts
ambrosial airs o'er milky billows and psalmy waves, to mingle with the
syllabl'ing matins and impassion the sighs of voluptuous maidens in their
bowers. This "literary language" could not have been more alien to the
geographical and cultural realities of nineteenth-century North America. It
was commonly used, however, if not usually in such affluence, by minor
poets (and some not-so-minor ones) on both sides of the Atlantic in
Sangster's time.

The poem is "imitative"—or "slavish," as Dudek puts it. Of course, as
Dudek allows, Sangster cannot be denounced for employing the Spenserian stanza as such, unless we are prepared to extend the denunciation to
include Byron, Keats, Burns, and a goodly number of other poets who
used it. The fact that Sangster borrowed not only the stanza, but the basic
concept of the poem from Byron is where the imitativeness begins, but it
does not end there. He borrowed many phrases with their associations
intact from other poets, and he borrowed ideas beyond the basic one from
Byron. We have already seen examples of phrases borrowed from Tennyson, Coleridge, Milton, and other poets, and scores of other examples
could be cited. It will be evident, for instance, that the following passages
echo lines from Wordsworth, Byron, and Scott, respectively:

> Beneath me, the vast city lay at rest;
> Its great heart throbbing gently. [XXXIX]

> Roll on in all thy mystery and might! [LXXVIII]

Is there soul so dead to nature's charms,
That thrills not here in this divine retreat? [C]

The commentators would not seem to be in agreement about Sangster's handling of the Spenserian stanzas. While Smith says that they are "skilfully handled," Dudek finds them to be "mechanical." It can hardly be said that they are skillfully handled mechanically. Technically speaking, no doubt, Stewart describes the stanzas as "uncouth"; Pierce, as "faulty." Baker notes the "false rhymes." While Sangster never actually deviates from the Spenserian *rhyme scheme*, there are *imperfect rhymes* in almost a third of the stanzas; for example: soars/towers, appear/worshipper, chief/cliff, song/among, love/remove, strewn/alone, terraces/these, upon/stone, lord/stirred, sun/moon, and hath/scathe. Bourinot is closer to the real technical problem when he refers to the rhythm as being "weak" and "faulty." Sangster deviates from the iambic foot in a majority of the stanzas and frequently from the pentameter line (he takes more care with the hexameters). The following passage illustrates both types of deviation as well as the ineffectual result:

Through the dense air the terror striken clouds
Fly, tortured by the pursuing hurricane.
Fast bound the milky billows—the white shrouds
That wind around the mariner on the main. [XVI]

Turning to the positive commentary, Wilson finds the poem "pleasant" and "tasteful"; Stewart finds it "admirable"; and Baker states that Sangster has a "feeling for nature." Speaking more specifically, Baker applies the word "felicitous" to the phrasing; Bourinot, the word "memorable." Pacey finds some of the descriptive passages to be "well-observed." It is in the descriptive passages primarily that we see evidence of poetic strength. Sangster had a painter's eye, though he did not often use it. Some of the description is in simple, nonfigurative language. In the following lines, he describes the rural countryside near Quebec City:

The corn
Upon the distant fields was ripe. Away
To the far left the swelling highlands lay;
The quiet cove, the river, bright and still. [LII]

He observes flocks of waterfowl rise from the surface of the lake at the Thousand Islands:

> Up start large flocks of waterfowl, that shake
> The spray from their glossed plumage, as they fly
> To seek the shelter of some island brake. [XIV]

In the following passage, spring is personified and the description is more elaborate. The observation is again accurate, and thought, language, and rhythm (though technically faulty again) harmonize nicely to make this one of the most esthetically appealing stanzas in the poem:

> The Spring is gone—light, genial-hearted Spring!
> Whose breath gives odor to the violet,
> Crimsons the wild rose, tints the blackbird's wing,
> Unfolds the buttercup. Spring that has set
> To music the laughter of the rivulet,
> Sent warm pulsations through the hearts of hills,
> Reclothed the forests, made the valleys wet
> With pearly dew, and waked the grave old mills
> From their calm sleep. . . . [XII]

He often exhibits refreshing originality in the use of simile and metaphor:

> A playful waterfall comes dashing down,
> As silvery as the laughter of a child
> Dancing upon the greensward, and the sun
> Scatters his golden arrows through the wild. [XCIX]

> And Darkness, like a Fate, comes stealing down
> In her black mantle, step by step, until
> The trembling stars have dwindled down to one
> Pale, solitary watcher. . . . [LXXII]

Many other examples could be used. He speaks of the "silver-sinewed arms of the proud lake"; a rock leaps "glowing from the deep abyss, on wings of fire"; and the evening star comes into the sky "like a chrysalis that has burst its tomb."

E. H. Dewart, himself an adornment to Canada's literary history, speaks favorably of the lyrics in "The St. Lawrence and the Saguenay," and so do several of the other commentators. Baker, curiously, dismisses them as lacking "spontaneity and grace." If the greatest facility which Sangster shows in the poem is for effective description, his secondary gift is for melody. Baker's statement could apply with justice to some of the lyrics but surely not to most of them; certainly not to the "Lyric to the Isles."

The language of this lyric is old-fashioned, but in this case the words are only of secondary importance. What matters is the melody, and it rises as elegantly here as in any poem of Sangster's:

> Here the Spirit of Beauty keepeth
>   Jubilee for evermore;
> Here the Voice of Gladness leapeth,
>   Echoing from shore to shore.
> O'er the hidden watery valley,
>   O'er each buried wood and glade,
> Dances our delighted galley,
>   Through the sunlight and the shade—
> Dances o'er the granite cells,
>   Where the Soul of Beauty dwells.

In summary, "The St. Lawrence and the Saguenay" is the work of a man of marked ability, but it is not in any sense of the term a successful "work of art." It lacks unity; it is technically wanting; and it is imitative and pretentious. But the whole is somehow greater than the sum of its parts. Maybe it is the great river itself which transcends the poem; maybe it is the dignity which the poet brings to a noble subject; or maybe it is the realization that beneath the surface of this poem lie the dead dreams of epic journeys and great spiritual struggles. Whatever the reason, the poem is, in its way, very grand.

V Bertram and Lorenzo

The lengthiest of the eighty-two "other poems" in *The St. Lawrence and the Saguenay* is "Bertram and Lorenzo—A Dramatic Fragment," a work of some seven hundred lines. This "fragment" is written in blank verse and is presented in the form of a play. There are three scenes, each involving dialogue between the two characters named in the title: Bertram, a gay, young university man; and Lorenzo, who is known as the Hermit of the Hills. Lorenzo, to use Sangster's preferred term, is an "enthusiast." His philosophy, which prevails in the poem, is that God is manifested in nature and that nature is the proper guide to man's emotional and spiritual being. The poem is, in fact, Sangster's most forthright and extensive statement on this subject.

The setting of Scene One is described as follows: "A picturesque Valley. A range of Mountains in the background. Cascade, falling into a waveless Lake at the base of the Cliff. Time, Evening." Bertram begins: "This is a lonely place." And, in reply, Lorenzo launches at once into the subject of communion with nature:

> Call it not lonely;
> Say, rather, that the God of Nature hath
> Peopled these wilds with spiritual forms
> With which the man of an exhalted mind
> Can hold sweet converse in his studious hours.

Lorenzo holds forth for a page and a half in this vein, describing the life and beauty surrounding them on the mountain, before Bertram has an opportunity to protest: "Give me the town,/Old man; its gay delights are more to me/Than all the paltry beauties of this place." To which Lorenzo replies: "Give me the place where I can hold communion/With Nature and with Nature's God. . . ." Lorenzo is not prepared to concede any of Bertram's points. He speaks of the peace to be found in nature, of the many evidences of God's presence, and of his concept of striving toward perfection hand in hand with nature. Bertram appears to be almost equally obstinate. He says:

> Why! I would rather tread the pleasing halls,
> Where such light-hearted fellows as myself
> Had learned to kill the pleasure-winged hours
> With dance and song, than listen to the ravings
> Of an enthusiast. . . .

In early youth, says Lorenzo, he shared in all the joys which Bertram has mentioned "but took no real pleasure from them." He convinces Bertram to climb with him to the top of the mountain, where he hopes to be able to prove to him that "God sits throned upon these lofty wilds." "Age has its whims," says Bertram, "to which youth must knuckle," and so he reluctantly agrees to follow Lorenzo up the mountain.

Scene Two is set "Midway up a rugged Mountain." The pathway is "rough and wearisome," and Bertram, the effete young man of the town, complains that he is tired. Lorenzo, an "enthusiast" all the way, utters a fitting homily: "Rebellious boy! dost think/The things that are worth seeking for/Can be procured without a little trouble?" At this point, several excruciatingly noble Wordsworthian peasants enter. They are also, of course, "enthusiasts" to the bone. The First Peasant calls the attention of his fellows to the sunset: "See, brothers, how the red-hot sun goes down,/Burning a steep path through the hissing wave,/That flames around him with the torrid heat." The Second Peasant acknowledges that it is indeed a "blessed sight," but then there is a sudden thunderclap, and the peasants have to hurry along to their "homes and happy hearths." These peasants, says Lorenzo, are "as happy fellows as the sun e'er shone on."

They continue their climb, Lorenzo readily finding words with which to counter all of Bertram's arguments.

Scene Three: "The summit of a high mountain looking Westward—Time, Sunset." "Hark! " says Lorenzo, "the thunder," and they go to the verge of the peak to observe the storm. Lorenzo lectures Bertram throughout the storm, calling his attention to the "passionate clouds" which "struggle like giant wrestling-groups" and to a wide range of other natural phenomena. Finally, Bertram yields:

> I can now discern
> How such a soul as thine is elevated
> Above the world and its ephemeral pleasures.
> Henceforward I'll participate with thee
> In these ethereal blessings. . . .

Until now, Bertram has not known the true identity of his companion. To him, he has been simply the old Hermit of the Hills, as he was known to the mountain peasants. Now that Bertram has been gathered into the fold, the Hermit dramatically removes his disguise and proclaims: "Thy youthful friend, whom thou didst call a bookworm! "

As we saw in Chapter 3, Sangster successfully dissuaded his friends from proposing him as a candidate for an honorary degree from Queen's, stating that this sort of thing was not in his line. We credited him with modesty for this attitude, but if we are to take the concluding lines of "Bertram and Lorenzo" seriously, arrogance may have been the real basis for his qualms. Lorenzo is going to school Bertram in the ways of nature:

> You will commence your schooling, and become
> My fellow-student. Nature for our guide,
> Depend upon it we will learn far more
> Than any pair of beardling adepts did
> In those cold, formal universities,
> Where young men's heads were crammed like Christmas turkeys,
> Making them passive as a sweating group
> Of listless Dutchmen o'er their meerschaum pipes
> That deaden all their faculties of mind.

It is ironic to reflect on what fate might long since have befallen Sangster's threadbare volumes had it not been for the tending given them by various "beardling adepts" in those "cold, formal universities."

Critical commentary on the title poem is sparse; on "Bertram and Lorenzo" it is virtually nonexistent. It would seem that George Stewart was the only person ever to review the poem in print, which he did in his

1869 essay on Sangster. Since Stewart's review has almost as much unpremeditated amusement value as the poem itself has, it is worth quoting in part:

Sangster's first volume closes with an attempt at dramatic composition. This fragment is entitled "Bertram and Lorenzo." The language used is for the most part good. Some very excellent ideas are put into the mouths of the speakers and a happy conceit pervades the whole. . . .

Bertram is a young and frivolous youth who possesses a soul for gaiety alone. Lorenzo is also young but is studious and somewhat philosophical in his nature. He likes amusements; but takes them in moderation. He has a strange and curious fancy to ascend mountains in the disguise of an old man. With the villagers he freely mingles, and they have learned to love and revere him. . . . Bertram is his friend. One day in disguise he sought him and the twain climb the heights together. The young man with that peculiar smartness characteristic of the "young man of the period" tries to outwit his aged companion with the cuteness of his sayings; but the "old fox" is too much for him, and he invariably gets the worst of it. The *incognito* of Lorenzo is preserved until the close of the last scene. Lorenzo speaks of his own happiness in leading the life he does and implores Bertram to imitate him. But the youth afraid that he must give up all the pleasures of the world, refuses to do so and asks

> "Must I relinquish all the harmless pleasures,
> That I had previously indulged in? "

"No," is the answer, but "use them in moderation."

>   "I would not ask
> That thou should'st ape the moody devotee,
> And live apart from all thy fellow men.
> For rather would I have thee still remain
> A trifling mortal, pleased with empty show,
> And gilded vanity, than encourage thee
> To be a soulless hermit."

There is something Shakespearian in the logic of these words. It is truly a brilliant sentence.

George Stewart, the only Canadian of his day who could claim membership in the International Literary Congress of Europe, saw Lorenzo's nature worship merely as "a strange and curious fancy to ascend mountains in the disguise of an old man" and a few flat lines as "brilliant" and "Shakespearian"!

Desmond Pacey comes much closer to the truth in describing this poem as "almost utterly without merit." Although it represents Sangster's most elaborate statement of commitment to the ethos of the Romantic poets, there is no profundity in the work, and the obvious is rather grievously belabored. The poem is highly artificial and quite offensively didactic. The blank verse is flat, and it prevents Sangster from exercising his lyrical facility, just as the didactic purpose and the dialogue format inhibit him from writing effective description. A few images, such as the following, stand out: "The moon, like a royal traveller,/Her silver chariot axle-deep in stars/Rides the burning labyrinth of worlds." More frequent, however, are ridiculous lines such as this: "He had great soul-thoughts floating in his eyes." Sangster obviously did not feel comfortable working within the restrictions imposed by this form, and he did not attempt any more "dramas." We leave "Bertram and Lorenzo" with a deep sense of gratitude that it came to no more than a fragment.

VI *Nature Poems*

About a quarter of the eighty-one shorter poems in the volume might be described as nature poems. Some of these are purely descriptive; others are basically religious. One of the most satisfying of the religious nature poems is "Sun, Moon, and Stars." In this poem, Sangster sees God as supreme over all creation and sees man, by contrast, as a mere atom:

> And how shall I, an atom, frail and weak,
>   Scan the blue ether with an eye of love,
> Or in befitting accents sing or speak
>   Of those mysterious worlds that shine above?
> But thou hast planted deep within my breast
>   A love for all that's beautiful and bright,
> From the red Morning's Sun-emblazoned crest,
>   To the pale stars that celebrate the Night.

God has given his secrets to nature, and man should turn to nature to read God's works. Sangster asks God to strengthen his understanding and love of creation, so that he may better serve Him:

> Teach me, Oh! God, to read thy works aright,
>   Fill me with love for all things bright and free,
> Grant me, through life to look, by day and night,
>   Through all Thy vast creations up to Thee!

The thought is conventional here, as it is in all of Sangster's work, but in general it is both attractively and convincingly expressed.

In "The Voice of God," a somewhat weaker poem, the same thought is present. All creation testifies to God's supremacy and sings His praises.

The St. Lawrence and the Saguenay

The following lines, in which Sangster pictures the creation of the heavenly bodies, when God summoned order out of chaos, are not without power:

> They sprang ablaze with their redundant light,
> While angels sped from orb to orb, and viewed
> The gleaming worlds, where all was solitude;
> And awed to silence, gazed with wonder on
> Each blazing planet and impassioned sun;
> Saw the swift meteor urge its burning car
> Adown the breathless silences afar,
> And watched the advent of each new-born star,
> Bursting the blue enamel of the sky,
> As it came clothed with splendor from on high,
> Launched on its errand of infinity!

A less ambitious poem of three stanzas entitled "The Whirlwind" is similar in tone, although it is strictly descriptive. The poem is marred by a flat stanza at the end, but the first stanza is worth quoting as an example of Sangster's vigorous treatment of the cataclysmic aspect of nature:

> It comes with its swift, destructive tread,
>   It tosses the waves on high,
> And it hurries away where the lightnings play,
>   Through the black and frowning sky;
> And the weeping clouds are madly driven
> By its violent breath, o'er the face of heaven.

"A Morning in Summer" is an interesting poem composed of some two hundred and twenty-five lines of blank verse. It has strong religious overtones, but it is not primarily a religious poem. It opens with a description of the coming of dawn, which Sangster so frequently describes in terms of all of the stars save one (Venus) having disappeared from the sky. In the following lines, dawn gives way to morning in splendid imagery:

> The silver dawn flies up the dusky slope,
> Like a white dove emerging from a cloud;
> Morning imprints its first impassioned kiss
> Upon the Orient's lips. . . .

With the arrival of morning, human life stirs, morning prayers are offered, and from the "gorgeous East" the chariot of the Godlike sun mounts the sky. The poet pauses to wonder in rather vital language over the mystery of the sun:

> Who filled the measure of thy beams, O Sun?
> Who took thee from the flaming womb of night,
> To be a wonder to all coming time?
> Who opened up the fountains of thy light?
> Who fashioned thee with splendor and with strength,
> And sent thee forth on thy victorious way?
> What star first paled to thy superior light?
> What human eye first drooped beneath thy gaze?
> What human voice first broke upon thine ear?
> What spot of earth first felt thy warming rays?

The morning sun turns the vegetation green and crimsons the cheek of the maiden. It brings the husbandman out to the fields. An idyllic village scene is painted, and the poet's tone conveys his admiration for the simple world and the "natural" people he is picturing. Then, suddenly, the peace is shattered by the roar and clatter of the "iron horse":

> Anon he comes,
> The massive giant, his o'erheated sides
> Reeking with sweat, and from his nostrils wide
> His heavy breathings issuing, in a cloud
> Of boiling vapor. Swiftly he glides past,
> Shuffling with half-majestic carelessness,
> With haughty ease, and time-defying pace,
> Until his race is run. Behold him now,
> Pawing the ground, impetuous in his haste
> To end his swift career. . . .

Logically, we would expect Sangster to depict the train as a symbol of destruction and corruption, but not so. The train brings "stores of wealth" to fight the "haggard creature want." Gladness brightens the faces of the villagers. The train symbolizes the march of civilization:

> His own career is onward, like the march
> Of a great conquerer; and by his strength
> He rushes boldly through the serried ranks
> Of the deep forest; ignorance disappears;
> Barrenness flies, screaming, to the ridgy steep,
> And Civilization triumphs in his wake.

The St. Lawrence and the Saguenay

The train gone, the Wordsworthian world is restored, and the account of the morning ends as the "oppressive hour of scorching noon" approaches. While we find here, as Lord Durham might have said, two concepts warring in the bosom of a single theme, we also find some of Sangster's most majestic lines. The poem has been ignored so far by anthologists; it deserves a second look.

Another interesting nature poem is "Autumn," an odelike poem in which Sangster depicts autumn as a pacifier and purifier. "A Plea for the Woods," one of three "woods" poems in the volume, illustrates Sangster's acceptance (or aping, as the case may be) of Wordsworth's belief in the restorative power of nature. Two poems describing lake scenes are weak. In "Evening Scene," for example, which is descriptive of Lake Erie after sunset, there are eighteen quatrains filled with "trembling" poplars, "stately" walnuts, "graceful" elms, "energetic" oaks, "red-leafed" maples, "slender" pines, "juicy" apples, "mellow" pears, "downy" peaches, and so on. The poem also contains the saddest example in Sangster of what might be called poetic vandalism. The fragile associations of Keats's "Ode to Autumn" are laid waste by a "young urchin" lolling on the grass, thinking of "Autumn with her red-ripe store." The other of the lake poems, "Rideau Lake," presents a morning scene, and while the language is not quite as conventional as that in "Evening Scene," we do encounter "stately cedars" and "sunny verdure." The misty silence of the dawn—one of Sangster's favorite moods—is well captured, but the triplet which he employs makes the rhythm jerky. The poem ends with day breaking: "The leaves like woodland pulses shake,/The plover whistles in the brake,/Wide day sits crowned on Rideau Lake."

" 'Pleasant Memories,' " said the New York *Albion*, in its review of *The St. Lawrence and the Saguenay*, "is original and excellent." The poem also appealed to Arthur S. Bourinot. " 'Pleasant Memories,' " he wrote, "is well named. It is a nostalgic poem, perhaps a trifle too sentimental, but for all that pleasing and of an interesting rhythm. The phraseology is simpler than in some of the other verses and more suitable to the theme." The poem is presented in the form of questions to "Mary" about the past:

> Mary, do you remember—
> Do you remember the ancient house,
> The moss to its brown roof clinging—
> The old open roof, where the swallows each year
> Reared their downy broods, without let or fear—
>   The moss in the eaves,
>   And the birds 'mong the leaves. . . .

This is common, sentimental verse, but it is easier to take than much of Sangster's writing.

Finally, "The Frost King's Revel," a blank-verse poem of more than two hundred lines, is of some interest. The Frost King is the personification of winter, and the poem is seminarrative. Sangster profoundly disliked winter and frequently pictured it as tyrannous. The Frost King is a killer assisted by personified winds that pierce and freeze the marrow of men's bones. His schemes are cruel, and his hands are deathly. He strikes a mother and baby fleeing from their burning home, a traveler trapped by an avalanche, and a "happy swain and affianced bride" whose sleigh breaks through the river ice. He gleefully assaults a drunkard emerging from "some vile brothel, rank with pestilence"; he had long had his eye on "this senseless and inebriated fool." The poem is of particular interest because of its depiction of nature as a malignant force, in contrast with Sangster's usual attitude of nature worship. Even the stars in the winter sky "flash hatred at each other." Here are the opening lines of the poem:

> It was a night of terror—fiercely bleak!
> The winds like haggard demons leaped along
> The whitened fields. Far o'er the piney hills,
> Far up among the mountain fastnesses,
> Their horrid laughter and avenging tones,
> Shook the red granite to its base. The trees
> Sprang from the frozen ground in fear, and fell
> Death-doomed to earth.

As a whole, the nature poems in the first volume can still be read with enjoyment. It is true that most of the poems are marred by stock diction, faulty rhythm, and other conspicuous imperfections, but there is an abundance of colorful imagery to be found, and some of the passages have an almost Miltonic stateliness.

VII *Love Poems*

There are more than twenty pieces which could be classified as love poems, and, as stated earlier, some commentators on Sangster claim that love is the dominant theme of the volume. A favorite idea of these love poems is that earth is not really a suitable place for love. In at least three of the poems, Sangster proffers his affections with an expression of the wish that consummation take place in heaven. This variety of platonic love is celebrated in "Beyond the Grave" (where, it must be admitted, there is some confusion as to whether the one addressed is living or dead), "Annie

By My Side is Sitting," and "I Dreamed I Met Her." None of these poems is especially meritorious, but "I Dreamed I Met Her" is the best of the three, and the following stanza from it illustrates both the thought common to all of these poems and the manner in which the thought is expressed:

> Thus would I meet thee, fairest one!
> If there the power should be given
> To know each other, where the Sun
> Of Love forever shines, in Heaven.
> Oh! joy beyond what earth can give!
> To see thee and to know thee, where
> The good in endless pleasures live—
> 'Twere heaven, indeed, if thou wert there.

Another poem, entitled "Love's Signet Ring," while not voicing the same thought, is ambiguous on the subject of sexual love versus heavenly love. Love of woman and love of God are so confused that it is not possible to determine to whom many of the lines are addressed.

Perhaps the most interesting of the love poems in the volume, though, from the point of view of idea, is a sequence of five sonnets entitled "Sonnet," "Hope," "The Trio," "The One Idea," and "Uncurbed Passion." These sonnets suggest a conflict within the poet between the dictates of his emotions and his idealization and idolization of love—as best exemplified by his desire to make love in heaven. In the first sonnet, he tells his dark-eyed one that she is the embodiment of his long-cherished ideal of beauty and that she will remain the embodiment of this ideal forever. The theme of "Hope," the second sonnet, is that love is a wellspring of hope:

> Where'er she smiles the landscape wears a glow
> Of calm serenity. Her skill doth blend
> Heaven's hues with those of earth. Weak and undone
> Were man, without the gift of the Eternal One.

The "trio" are love, hope, and "that deceitful elf called sorrow," which always walks hand in hand with love. Love is not all good, however. In "The One Idea," love is a tyrant:

> Oh! how it burns the brain, and tramples down
> All other thoughts that struggle to be freed
> From their imprisonment, driving them back

> With its stern mandate, or its sterner frown. . . .
> This reigning thought, which liveth there enshrined!
> Thoughts that did once at my mere bidding move,
> Are now the vassals of the tyrant—Love!

Love, the tyrant, arouses passion as strong as "a human Niagara" or "an alpine avalanche." And passion, to Sangster, is not merely tyrannous; it is contrary to reason, sinful, and ruinous, as he makes clear in the final sonnet in the sequence:

> The unchained bolt
> Of sin's dread electricity. The revolt
> Of judgment. Agent of the arch-traitor's frown.
> The midnight tempest on a stormy sea.
> Reason's eclipse. The Mephistophiles
> That points the murderer's weapon: Like to these,
> And in its headlong fury ever thus,
> Is Passion unrestrained: The simoom's breath—
> The entrance to the whirlpool, and to death.

A number of the shorter love lyrics in the volume are unpretentious and quite engaging. Typical of these is "Love's Morning Lark." In the first stanza of this one, Sangster describes the lark as the bright-winged herald of the dawn; in the second, he asks his maiden to be his lark of love:

> So, Maiden, thou shalt be the Lark,
>   And I, the long-expectant Morn;
> Bring back the lost Dove to its Ark,
> And let my mateless heart be bless'd,
> My being in thy soul find rest,
>   And my new life be Music-born.

"Love's New Era" is similar both in theme and execution. "The Impatient Lover" is more conventional but not at all unpleasant. Less successful are "Imagination," a longer poem, and "Absence," fourteen lines of weary verse in which the poet longs for the return of his love. "Love's Guiding Star," another poem on the subject of love lost, is a cheerless exercise indeed:

> No guiding star to cheer me onward,
>   To wing my better thoughts to God,
> But dark despair impels me downward,
>   I see my grave beneath the sod!

The concept of "Aurelia," which is over a hundred and fifty lines in length, is pleasant enough. Aurelia is fairer, but only barely so, than Amelia, Hatty, Libby, Louisa, Annie, or Caroline, to each of whom eight lines of praise are devoted. However, the diction is inflated, and some distressing lapses in taste occur. "The Betrayal," "A Thousand Faces," and "Pretty Faces" are all utterly trivial. The following stanza from "Pretty Faces" is perhaps not the worst one which could be quoted:

> Where the lips are slightly pouting,
>   Where the full, dark eye, is bright—
> Bright and soft as morn and even—
>   Bright and dark as noon and night.

Surely one of the silliest poems which Sangster ever wrote is "The Name of Mary," which was probably written for Mary Kilborn, his bride-to-be at this time:

> Most welcome, though, to English ears,
>   Fit for a throned Queen or graceful Fairy,
> Is that sweet household word that bears
>   The sound of—MARY.
>
> It mingles with our childhood's games
>   It chastens either birth or bridal;
> Mary! to me the very name's
>   A perfect Idyl.

In general, in this first volume, we see Sangster idealizing love but disdaining passion. Often his love mood is melancholy, but we also catch him writing giddy little rhymes about women's names and faces. In rare moments, he is capable of writing love lyrics in the spirit, if not with the gracefulness, of Burns. The love poems provide some insights into Sangster's character, but there is little here of literary worth. Neither do these love poems, in comparison with the nature poems, provide a sound basis for the claim that love is the dominant theme of the volume.

VIII *Miscellany*

W. D. Lighthall put his finger on the problem and perhaps the cause of the problem which bedevils many of Sangster's introspective poems when he wrote of Sangster: "Defective education in youth deprived him of the resources of modern art ... making a good deal of his poetry the curious spectacle of inborn strivings after perfect ideals driven to expression in abstractions rather than in concrete clothing of colours and forms." In the discussion of the title poem, we observed something both of Sangster's fondness for abstract concepts and his ineptness in handling them. It is in the introspective, or "soul" poems that we often see this problem in sharpest focus. Seemingly subject throughout his life to periods of melancholy and depression, he sought relief through cataloging his woes in verse, with the result that the introspective poems tend to be morbid as well as abstruse.

Perhaps the most successful of the introspective poems is "Despondency," a sonnet. E. H. Dewart well described its effectiveness, in the following words: "Though evidently the product of a morbid mental mood, it has a weird intensity of emotion in it, which makes it hard for one to read it without feeling something of the cowering dread which it describes." The poem speaks for itself:

> I feel the germs of madness in me springing,
> Slowly, and certain, as the serpent's bound,
> And my poor hopes, like dying tendrils clinging
> To the green oak, tend surely to the ground. . . .
> And the bright taper Hope once fed within
> Hath waned and perished in the rueful din.

There are two other introspective sonnets—"Light in Darkness," and "Remembrances." The former has the distinction, among Sangster's sonnets, of having an almost perfect Shakespearian rhyme scheme. It is very sluggish, however, containing such passages as "a double darkness dread/ Englooms my spiritual sense." "The Past," which has two sonnetlike stanzas, is not quite as morose as most of the others. On "Soul, Thou Art Lonely" and "Peace Fond Soul," we should, in justice, accept Sangster's own latter-day verdict. "The two poems on the Soul," he said, "are nonsense."[10]

By the time his poetic activity finally lumbered to a halt, Sangster had written quite a number of poems on death. "Fanny," for instance, was written on the death of the wife of one of his brothers, and, as he later allowed, it is "imperfect." It lacks restraint in its description of the "dismal coffin and the shroud," but a few of its lines are clean: "Along the straight and dusty road,/And through the shadowy groves of pines/The lone procession moves and twines." "Little Annie" is sentimental, as most of the poems on death are:

> How mildly passed her second birth,
> How sweet the assurance given:

> One Angel less upon the earth,
>   One Spirit more in heaven!
> We knew she was a tender flower,
>   Dropped, but not planted here,
> And, knowing, feared the coming hour,
>   Too bitter for the tear
> That grief itself had not the power
>   To shed upon her bier.

"Gentle Mary Ann" is similar, and it is also rhythmically faulty. Two occasional verses on the passing of clergymen—"To Rev. James G. Witted" and "Elegy in Memory of Rev. Robert D. Cartwright"—are of little interest. In "Henry's Grave" are lines which read: "My vision seemed to fail," and "All became confused as blackest night." Certainly, the poems on death in this volume have little light to shed on the subject.

"Mr. Sangster," says George Stewart, "writes a capital song. . . . This form of poetical composition, unless well done should never be attempted. 'The Heroes of the Alma' and 'The Banner of Old England' are very good and so is an Alma lyric, 'The Two-Fold Victory.' " "The Heroes of the Alma" is a spirited martial song; "The Two-Fold Victory" is a brief narrative poem about a soldier who died just as victory came in the Crimean War. "The Banner of Old England" is a birthday song for Queen Victoria; its first stanza is typical of the spirit and quality of the patriotic songs in the volume:

> Raise high the broad Banner!
> Old England's broad Banner!
> That waves its Red Cross over every sea;
>   With hearts firm and loyal,
>   Cheer loud for the Royal—
> The famed Royal Standard, the Flag of the Free!

The only patriotic poem having to do specifically with Canada is "From Queenston Heights," a poem presented from the point of view of a letter or report on a visit to Queenston Heights, where General Sir Isaac Brock died in battle during a successful repulse of an American force in the War of 1812: "Here is the monument. Immortal Brock,/Whose ashes lie beneath it, not more still/Than is the plain today." Although Sangster writes stirring martial songs, he does not glory in the thought of war:

> What have we gained,
> But a mere breath of fame, for all the blood
> That flowed profusely on this stirring field?

'T is true, a Victory; through which we still
Fling forth the meteor banner to the breeze,
And have a blood-sealed claim upon the soil.

He has great admiration for the "Old Land," and he does not think that provocation by the United States should be tolerated, but his fundamental loyalty is to British traditions and British "blood," rather than to the state of Great Britain, and he actually pities himself for his pride in Brock who, after all, defeated his own "brothers":

My Brothers all, Vanquished and Victors both,
And yet my heart leaps up, poor human heart!
As I lean proudly, with a human pride,
Against this pillar to a great man's name.

Sangster's love for both Great Britain and the United States and his desire for them to stand united is best expressed in "England and America," a poem which R. P. Baker says "is sufficient to make *The St. Lawrence and the Saguenay* an interesting volume." Here are the opening stanzas:

Greatest twain among the nations,
Bound, alike, by kindred ties—
Ties that never should be sundered
While your banners grace the skies—
But, united, stand and labor,
Side by side, and hand in hand,
Battling with the sword of Freedom,
For the peace of every land.

Yours the one beloved language,
Yours the same religious creed,
Yours the glory and the power,
Great as ever was the need
Of old Rome, or Greece, or Sparta,
When their arms victoriously,
Proved their terrible puissance
Over every land and sea.

The fantastic type of thing with which we are faced in the didactic verses is exemplified by the first stanza from "Password—Truth is Mighty":

Stand not on the Alps of Error,
Brother, though the tempting height

> Lure thee to the grassy hill-top,
>   Though the view enchant the sight;
> But if sorely tempted thither,
>   In some hour of gilded woe,
> Stand, and gaze around thee, Brother,
>   On the Vale of Truth below.

In a similar self-righteous spirit is "The Lofty and the Lowly," which was probably inspired by Burns's "For A' That and A' That" and "Let Them Boast as They Will," which is critical of the world's "giddy pleasures." Even these, however, do not equal "Pity's Tear Drop":

> As Pity looked down from on high,
>   So smilingly, sweetly, and meek,
> A tear-drop that stood in her eye
>   Fell on a drunkard's cheek.
>
> Astonished, he looked above,
>   Not a star overhead could he see;
> He said: "'Tis a tear-drop of love
>   Shed by my Ella for me."

Alcohol is not Sangster's portion, as he makes clear again in another dreadful verse entitled "The Grape." But, in fairness, it should be noted that he himself came to loathe these didactic verses. "When you meet with a little affair belonging to *The St. Lawrence and the Saguenay* called 'Pity's Tear Drop,' he wrote, to W. D. Lighthall, after he had deposited his manuscripts with him, "please to destroy the little piece of nonsense."[11]

Few other poems in the volume are deserving of mention. In "Snow Drops," children are described as "spotless human snow drops"—from which the tenor of the emotion can be gauged. But "Snow Drops" pales beside the puerility of "The Yellow Curl," which is prefaced by the statement, "I send you one of Little Libby's curls." "Festus" is a sonnet on P. J. Bailey's Faustlike work by that name. Sangster finds it "not strictly orthodox" but "brimming full of divinest meanings." To end on a better note, here is the second stanza of "My Kitten":

> Teasing, saucy little pest!
> Will you never be at rest?
> Romping in and out the house,
> Chasing tabby for a mouse,
> Climbing nimbly up the door,
> Strewing papers round the floor,
> Prancing up and down the roof,

Giving, every moment, proof
That all living things should strive
To be happy while alive.

IX *Conclusion*

Most of the reviews of *The St. Lawrence and the Saguenay* were, as we saw in Chapter 2, commendatory in the extreme. It was not long, however, until opinion sobered somewhat. E. H. Dewart later acknowledged that he found the volume to be "not uniform in merit throughout, and sometimes bearing marks of want of time for elaboration." H. J. Morgan saw it as "not generally distinguished for . . . artistic finish."[12] Sangster, always his own best critic, was so dissatisfied with it that he had prepared a revised edition (which was never published) by 1862 and some years later, in one of his letters, complained that the book "startled" him and made him "nervous."[13] Writing in 1920, R. P. Baker said that here was "little promise of ultimate achievement."

What, in summary, are the strengths and weaknesses of the volume? There is evidence in the title poem, and especially in the nature poems, of a gift for imagery. In these poems, there are lines and passages of genuine poetic power, but the pity is that Sangster is unable to control his talents. Inspiration comes to him sporadically, so that excellence is usually to be found side by side with banality. He is at his best in his nature descriptions, but even these are very uneven in merit. It is in the nature poems too (including the interludes in the title poem) that his gift for melody finds its most satisfying expression. His faults are innumerable. Almost all of his work is imitative to some extent; his diction is usually incongruous or hackneyed; his ideas are shallow, conventional, and poorly articulated; and he can often be annoyingly sentimental and didactic.

Speaking in terms of individual poems, what have we left after the dross is eliminated? We have a title poem, reduced to perhaps a third of its original length; we have all or parts of such nature poems as "Sun, Moon, and Stars," "The Voice of God," "Morning in Summer," and half a dozen of the purely descriptive pieces; and we have six or seven love lyrics, one or two patriotic poems, and a handful of minor verses such as "My Kitten." Speaking of the distorted critical reception given the book, R. P. Baker says: "With rare good sense, however, the *Criterion*, standing apart from the majority of periodicals, remarked that if Sangster had burned three-quarters of the contents and printed the remainder, he would have had an excellent volume. With this judgment few will take issue. . . . Sangster's fame depends on his second book."

CHAPTER 5

Hesperus

I *The Title Poem*

Even a glance through *Hesperus and Other Poems and Lyrics* (1860) reveals that this second volume differs markedly from the first one. It is a smaller book, containing seventy-five poems. Twenty-four of these are sonnets, and many of the others are short. The title poem, although it is a major piece of work, nearly six hundred lines in length, is not a poem of the magnitude of "The St. Lawrence and the Saguenay." The first title poem was Byronic; the second one is Miltonic, but in "Hesperus: A Legend of the Stars" Sangster is endeavoring to emulate the cosmic sweep of his great mentor rather than to imitate any specific poem. There are scattered echoes, it is true, of lines from "L'Allegro" and *Paradise Lost*, in particular, but rarely, if ever, are these as blatant as the echoes which are heard in "The St. Lawrence and the Saguenay."

In *The St. Lawrence and the Saguenay*, we saw that Sangster's attention was frequently caught by the planet Venus, as the morning or evening star—that "one pale solitary watcher," as he most memorably described it. In "Hesperus," he weaves a fanciful narrative about the origin of this, his favorite star. Written chiefly in blank verse, "Hesperus" is made up of a prelude and eight parts interspersed with lyrical "choruses." In the prelude, we are reminded that the stars, the "footprints" left by God when he created the universe, speak to the souls of all men about God's power and magnificence:

> The Stars are heaven's ministers;
> Right royally they teach
> God's glory and omnipotence
> In wondrous lowly speech.
> All eloquent with music as
> The trembling of a lyre;
> To him that hath an ear to hear
> They speak in words of fire.

The framework within which the narrative is set is that the poet and "Mary" are gazing on the evening star, when they are swept up into a dream world and across "seas of white vapor that whirled through skies afar," to where the celestial beings recount to them the story of the birth of Hesperus. The tale of fancy begins at the dawn of time, when there was harmony in heaven between God and his angels. It tells of the rebellion of Lucifer, of his banishment, with his followers, from paradise, and of the creation of the world:

> Then the hills
> Rose bald and rugged o'er the wild abyss;
> The waters found their places; and the sun,
> The bright-haired warder of the golden morn,
> Parting the curtains of reposing night,
> Rung his first challenge to the dismal shades.

God created the stars as memorials to the angels who were faithful to him. One seraph, the fairest in heaven, was chosen to lead all the others, and for him Hesperus, the star which leads the others into the evening sky, was created. In the concluding section of the poem, the watchers are returned to earth at dawn from their astral flight.

The following narrative passage, with the first stanza of a succeeding lyrical interlude, exemplifies the average quality of the verse:

> Innumerable multitudes and ranks
> Of all the hosts and hierarchs of heaven,
> Moved by one universal impulse, urged
> Their steeds to swiftness up the arch of light,
> From sphere to sphere increasing as they came,
> Till world on world was emptied of its race.
> Upward, with unimaginable speed,
> The myriads, congregating zenith-ward,
> Reached the far confines of the utmost sphere,
> The home of Truth, the dwelling-place of Love,
> Striking celestial symphonies divine
> From the resounding sea of melody,
> That heaved in swells of soft, mellifluous sound,
> To the blest crowds at whose triumphal tread
> Its soul of sweetness waked in thrills sublime.
> The sun stood poised upon the western verge;
> The moon paused, waiting for the march of earth,
> That stayed to watch the advent of the stars;
> And ocean hushed its very deepest deeps
>   In grateful expectation.

SECOND ANGEL
Still through the viewless regions
Of the habitable air,
Through the ether ocean,
In unceasing motion,
Pass the multitudinous legions
Of angels everywhere.

Sangster has disciplined himself better in this poem than he did in any poem in the first volume. The rhythms are regular; the melodies are true; and the diction, though lofty, is not incongruous. For all that, however, the reader is left with little when he finishes the poem. Sangster has taken a throttlehold upon his style, chastening it, to be sure, but at the same time choking the flow of natural color to his lines. Besides, even though the language itself is usually comprehensible, the diffuseness which characterized much of the first volume persists. The narrative is too thin to hold together a poem of eighteen pages, and it is seriously interrupted by the many lyrical interludes—no fewer than eleven of them—which are not closely related organically to the narrative. The poem leaves the reader with a pleasant impression of melody but also with a somewhat frustrating feeling of vacuity. The anonymous author of the article on Sangster in the old *Cyclopedia of Canadian Biography* made this point well, if a trifle quaintly: "Though Mr. Sangster took a high flight, aye, even to the stars, to grasp his subject—and though he may have grasped it in his own mind, he has failed to delineate it clearly.... It would be well if the young aspirant for the laurel-wreath would remember that poetic words thrown together promiscuously, or even with some attempt at form; aye, even with a perfect lyrical ring, will not make poetry, any more than a number of lovely tints, all in perfect harmony, thrown upon canvas will make a picture."[1] Still, if only for its technical superiority, "Hesperus: A Legend of the Stars" would have to be included in any collection of Sangster's best poems.

II *Two Idyls*

Desmond Pacey describes "Mariline" as "an idyll of country life, owing much of its music to Tennyson's 'Lady of Shalott' but set rather in an idealized present than in an idealized past." While the poem resembles "The Lady of Shalott" in rhyme and rhythm, it is not a slavish imitation (R. P. Baker sees the poem as imitative of Longfellow, for example). Tennyson employs a nine-line stanza rhyming, uniquely, *aaaabcccb*; Sangster uses alternative four- and two-line stanzas rhyming *aaaa bb*. The magic of Tennyson's music depends upon subtly blending variations (and constants) in meter and line within each stanza, as well as from stanza to stanza, although a majority of his lines do have eight syllables. Sangster's poem has a regular seven-syllable line, which is only one of a number of variant lines used, infrequently, by Tennyson in "The Lady of Shalott." The result is that, while Tennyson achieves a delicate union of rhythm and harmony, Sangster aims for, and gets, only a steady jogging rhythm and a simple melody.

"Mariline" resembles "The Lady of Shalott" in subject matter as well as in sound, but, once again, Tennyson's poem provided only the germ. Sangster's poem, which is nearly two hundred and fifty lines in length, is a seminarrative about Mariline's love for a scholarly shepherd lad. Winter is the season of the first part of the poem, in which we find Mariline plying the maidenly wheel:

> At the wheel plied Mariline
> Beauteous and self-serene
> Never dreaming of that mien
> Fit for lady or for queen.
>
> Never sang she but her words,
> Music-laden, swept the chords
>
> Of the heart, that eagerly
> Stored the subtle melody. . . .

Summer comes in one of the most striking images in Sangster's poetry: "Brightly broke the summer morn,/Like a lark from out the corn,—/Broke like joy just newly born. . . ."

The powerful concluding stanzas of the poem are worth quoting in full:

> Ye whose souls are strong and firm,
> In whom love's electric germ
>
> Has been fanned into a flame
> At the mention of a name;
> Ye whose souls are still the same
> As when first the Victor came,
>
> Stinging every nerve of life,
> In the beatific strife,
>
> Till the man's divinest part
> Ruled triumphant in the heart,

> And, with shrinking, sudden start,
> The bleak old world stood apart,
>
> Periling the wild Ideal
> By the presence of the Real:
>
> Ye, and ye alone, can know
> How these twain souls burn and glow,
> Can interpret every throe
> Of the full heart's overflow,
>
> That imparts that light serene
> To the brow of Mariline.

What strange, powerful lines these are! The poem has weak lines too, but generally speaking its expression is pure and elegant, making it one of Sangster's most attractive poems.

The second idyl, "The Happy Harvesters: A Cantata," is a poem of almost four hundred lines. Each of its seven parts is composed of a descriptive-narrative passage written in heroic couplets, and each part except the last one incorporates a lyric, song, or "ballad." The poem begins with a description of the autumn season and the happy harvesters. Fresh imagery, appropriate diction, and skillfully handled couplets make this Sangster's finest picture of autumn:

> Autumn, like an old poet in a haze
> Of golden visions, dreams away his days,
> So Hafiz-like that one may also hear
> The singer's thoughts imbue the atmosphere;
> Sweet as the dreamings of the nightingales
> Ere yet their songs have waked the eastern vales.
> Or stirred the airy echoes of the wood
> That haunt the forest's social solitude.

The harvesters, returning homeward after the day's work, sing an "Autumn Ode" which, once again, is one of Sangster's best hymnlike poems:

> God of the Harvest! Thou, whose sun
>   Has ripened all the golden grain,
> We bless thee for thy bounteous store,
> The cup of Plenty running o'er
>   The sunshine and the rain. . . .

Where'er the various-tinted woods,
　　In all their autumn splendor dressed,
Impart their gold and purple dyes
To distant hill and farthest skies
　　Along the crimson west:

Across the smooth, extended plain,
　　By rushing stream and broad lagoon,
On shady height and sunny dale,
Wherever scuds the balmy gale,
　　Or gleams the autumn moon. . . .

The inevitable "maid" of the idyl is introduced in very colorful heroic couplets:

Her gentle eyes serenest depths of blue
Shrined love and truth, and all their retinue;
The health and beauty of her youthful face
Made it the harem of each maiden grace;
And such perfection blended with her air,
She seemed some stately godess moving there.

Following the day's work, the harvesters enjoy an evening of gaiety:

From hand to hand the ripened fruit went round,
And rural sports a pleased acceptance found;
The youthful fiddler on his three-legged stool,
Fancied himself at least an Ole Bull;
Some easy bumpkin, seated on the floor,
Hunted the slipper till his ribs were sore.

And so to bed:

But soon the Morn, on many a distant height
Fingers the raven locks of lingering Night.

And the poem concludes with the start of a new day.

A number of commentators on Sangster have had praise for this idyl. George Stewart said it was "a cantata of much beauty." R. P. Baker found it "simple and unaffected," containing "many a realistic scene of the countryside." A. J. M. Smith says that passages such as the description of autumn and the introduction of the maid have "an old-fashioned artificial charm to which Sangster's fervid sensibility gives a warmth of feeling that is quite delightful." And Desmond Pacey notes the poem's similarity to Milton's "L'Allegro." Not only does "The Happy Harvesters" have much that is positive to recommend it, but it is an unusually even piece of writing, exhibiting few of Sangster's weaknesses. Looked at from either the positive or the negative standpoint, it is easily the most impressive of any of the lengthier works.

III *The Orillia Woods Sonnets*

A section of *Hesperus* is set specially aside for the sequence: "Sonnets Written in the Orillia Woods, August, 1859." It is obvious that most of the sonnets were written during an actual sojourn in the Orillia region. They are dedicated to "my friends at 'Rockridge,' Orillia, Canada West." Orillia is, of course, the town long since made famous by Stephen Leacock, and readers of *Sunshine Sketches of a Little Town* have a fond place in their hearts for it. Situated at the southern end of Lake Couchiching and near the head of Lake Simcoe, Orillia was in Sangster's day, even more than in Leacock's day or in our own, a pleasantly remote little place, surrounded by the deep woods of the northern half of Simcoe County. To the west, beyond the woods, is Georgian Bay, joined to Lake Couchiching by the Severn River. It was in this county—at Penetanguishene, on Georgian Bay—that Sangster's father died in 1824, a fact which may have attracted the poet to the area.

There are twenty-two sonnets (so called) in the sequence, as well as a prologue and an epilogue in blank verse. In the prologue, Sangster states his theory of nature as it applies to art, in the following terms: God is *truth* (also beauty, etc.); nature is the *soul of truth*; and art is the *spirit of truth*. All of his work is informed by the concept of the God-nature-art hierarchy, and he demonstrates elsewhere too that he had a Scholastic philosopher's penchant for the finer points of difference between the "soul" and the "spirit." He also visualizes his art as a means of serving God—through the improvment of his own mind: "I love my art; chiefly, because/Through it I rev'rence Nature, and improve/The tone and tenor of the mind he gave."

In more appealing lines, he describes his movements through the "Orillian" world:

> Out on the ever-changing Couchiching,
> By the rough margin of the Lake St. John;
> Down the steep Severn, where the artist sun,
> In dainty dalliance with the blushing stream,

Transcribes each tree, branch, leaf, and rock and flower,
Perfect in shape and color, clear distinct,
With all the panoramic change of sky. . . .

Nature promises to be the chief subject of the sonnets, but it proves to be by no means the only subject. There is a close resemblance between this sonnet sequence and "The St. Lawrence and the Saguenay." In both works, the world of nature through which the poet moves evokes from him a variety of poetic responses. He describes the character of the sequence well himself in the concluding lines of the prologue:

> And these leaves
> Of meditation are but perfumes from
> The censer of my feelings; honied drops
> Wrung from the busy hives of heart and brain;
> Mere etchings of the artist; grains of sand
> From the calm shores of that unsounded deep
> Of speculation, where all thought is lose
> Amid the realms of Nature and of God.

As we have seen, Sangster is interested not only in nature as it is, but in the origin of things. The mystery of creation fascinates him, and he frequently dreams of the cataclysms which, in eons past, gave birth to worlds. Seated on a rock in the Orillia woods in such a mood of wonder, he journeys back in imagination (assisted somewhat by Coleridge) through the geologic ages, to a time when God was shaping the woods which he is now enjoying, with the terrible forces of water and ice, and wrathful gale:

> Above where I am sitting, o'er these stones,
> The ocean waves once heaved their mighty forms,
> And vengeful tempests and appalling storms
> Wrung from the stricken sea portentous moans
> That rent stupendous icebergs, whose huge heights
> Crashed down in fragments through the startled nights. [VIII]

Ever mindful too of human history, he recalls that the Indians were the first possessors of these woods:

> My footsteps press where, centuries ago,
> The Red Men fought and conquered; lost and won.
> Whole tribes and races, gone like last year's snow,
> Have found the Eternal Hunting-Grounds, and run
> The fiery gauntlet of their active days. [XVI]

He often displays genuine sensitivity in his lines about the Indians: "A few sculls; a heap of human bones! / These are the records...."

As usual, though, Sangster is at his best in the present, describing the world around him. It is late summer:

> The birds are singing merrily, and here
> A squirrel claims the lordship of the woods,
> And scolds me for intruding. At my feet
> The tireless ants all silently proclaim
> The dignity of labor. In my ear
> The bee hums drowsily; from sweet to sweet
> Careering, like a lover weak in aim.
> I hear faint music in the solitudes;
> A dreamlike melody that whispers peace
> Imbues the calmy forest, and sweet rills
> Of pensive feeling murmur through my brain,
> Like ripplings of pure water down the hills
> That slumber in the moonlight. Cease, oh, cease!
> Some day my weary heart will coin these into pain. [IV]

Close observation of detail, appropriate diction, and true melody make this one of the best sonnets in the sequence. Its concluding image, in particular, is one of the most original in Sangster's poetry. Several of the other sonnets are comparable. The over-all effect of the descriptive narration in the following passage, for example, is most satisfying, even if we detect that the excellent opening line owes something to a line in *Childe Harold*:

> I've almost grown a portion of this place;
> I seem familiar with each mossy stone;
> Even the nimble chipmunk passes on,
> And looks, but never scolds me. Birds have flown
> And almost touched my hand; and I can trace
> The wild bees to their hives.... [XIII]

"Heart, mind and soul; I analysed them all," says Sangster, in one of the sonnets, and indeed many of them are introspective. Occasionally, his mood is optimistic: "I have grown/Full twenty summers backwards, and my youth/Is surging in upon me ..." [VI]. Typically, he feels blinded and lost: Our life is like a forest, where the sun/Glints down upon us through the throbbing leaves;/The full light rarely finds us..."[VII]. Usually he discovers that against his will his heart is busily coining his experiences into pain:

There is no sadness here. Oh, that my heart
Were calm and peaceful as these dreamy groves!
That all my hopes and passions, and deep loves,
Could sit in such an atmosphere of peace. [XIV]

"Bring back my olive branch of happiness, O dove! " he cries in one line, reclothing one of his favorite images. He has "fought with Sorrow face to face" and "tasted of the cup that brings to some/A frantic madness and delirious mirth." While he frequently indulges in the pathetic fallacy, interpreting nature in terms of his own emotion, he sometimes expresses his anguish directly, without recourse to analogy. In the following passage, he describes a "rough night" with chilling vividness:

                    All night long
My nerves were shaken, and my pulse stood still,
And waited for a terror yet to come
To strike harsh discords through my life's sweet song.
Sleep came—an incubus that filled the sum
Of wretchedness with dreams so wild and chill
That sweat oozed from me like great drops of gall;
An evil spirit kept my mind in thrall,
And rolled my body up like a poor scroll
On which is written curses that the soul
Shrinks back from when it sees some hellish carnival. [XV]

The religious theme is prominent in these sonnets, as it is in almost all of Sangster's poetry. He worships God through nature ("I go to worship in Thy House, O God!") and most of the sonnets end with a surge of religious sentiment. Two of them describe the blessings of rest, peace, and prayer which Sundays bring. There is also a furtive love theme: "The dawn/Of an imperishable love passed through/The lattice of my senses..." [XX]. But the talk of love never becomes explicit. Sangster never tells us who his companions were at "Rockridge" or who wandered with him through the Orillia Woods. We hear of the "friends" to whom he dedicates the sonnets, and the names of Alice, Carrie, and Eliza surface from time to time. He speaks of the "loving souls by whom I was surrounded" and of the fact that his companions regarded him at first as a dreamer. In the epilogue, it is "we" who depart from "Rockridge" with "parting words," "more lingering farewells," "pressure of hands," "the thrilling touch of lips," and "a waving of white handkerchiefs." The "fair Eliza" thinks the parting is "for the best," but, of course, we do not know who the fair Eliza is, whether she is leaving or staying, or who, in fact, is parting from whom. To wrap the mystery securely in an enigma, the epilogue ends with these lines:

> The city gas-lights flashed into our eyes;
> And we, half-shrinking from the glare and din
> Thought but of two more partings on the morn,
> When Love should be enfettered, hand and foot,
> For the long aeon of a human year.

Sangster and someone (or more) have reached a city—Toronto? Kingston? —on their journey from Orillia, and there are going to be two more partings in the morning which will enfetter somebody's love for a year. It would seem as though the prologue and epilogue were not only dedicated to friends but written exclusively for them.

Let us return to the last sonnet in the sequence to observe Sangster departing from the Orillia Woods under the influence of the pathetic fallacy:

> Dark, dismal day—the first of many such!
> The wind is sighing through the plaintive trees,
> In fitful gusts of a half-frenzied woe;
> Affrighted clouds the hand might almost touch,
> Their black wings bend so mournfully and low,
> Sweep through the skies like night-winds o'er the seas.
> There is no chirp of bird through all the grove,
> Save that of the young fledgling rudely flung
> From its warm nest; and like the clouds above
> My soul is dark, and restless as the breeze
> That leaps and dances over Couchiching.... [XXII]

Sangster was not a poet who understood the magic of place names—not as Bliss Carman understood their magic, nor even as E. J. Pratt did—but Couchiching is a name that Milton, in the stormy Hebrides of his imagination, might have admired; or wisest Keats, transfixed upon some glorious mountain top.

Technically speaking, the Orillia poems are not sonnets. They do have fourteen lines, and if we are willing to elide mentally as we read, most of them have thirteen iambic pentameter lines, but they end, it will have been noticed, with hexameters. The rhyme schemes range from no rhyme—or no scheme—through approximations of Spenserian and Shakespearian patterns to heroic couplets. The poems do not exhibit the compactness or exactness of expression characteristic of sonnets. They are simply fourteen-line poems, no better or no worse for being called sonnets.

There are quite a number of echoes from other poets in the sonnets, a few of which have been mentioned. Coleridge, Byron, and Tennyson are the most conspicuous sources, but there is an echo from Shakespeare's *Macbeth*, for instance, and this one from *The Tempest*: "the sacred fires/With which the other lighted up my mind/Have faded out and left no trace behind"[IX]. Some of these reworked lines definitely spoil the passages in which they occur. In other cases, however, Sangster is able to assimilate borrowed phrases in such a way that they enhance the effect which he is trying to achieve, beyond the humble capabilities of his own unaided imagination.

Although the sonnet sequence as a whole is marred by the spectrum of Sangster's abuses, we find here perhaps half a dozen of his best poems. Desmond Pacey cites the fourth, fifth, thirteenth, fourteenth, and twenty-second sonnets as the most successful. All, or part, of each of these is quoted above, as well as others which approach or equal them in quality.

IV *Into the Silent Land*

It will be recalled that Sangster's first wife, Mary Kilborn, died of pneumonia in 1858 at the age of twenty-two, little more than a year after their marriage. In *Hesperus*, published just two years after her death, Sangster devotes a special section entitled "Into the Silent Land" to her memory, although the section is not formally dedicated and her name does not appear. "Into the Silent Land" contains over eight hundred lines of verse. The first part is written in rhyming iambic pentameter lines and incorporates two lyrical pieces; the second part is composed of irregular rhyming lines and also incorporates two lyrics—"The Light in the Window Pane" and "The Soul." Sangster has made some attempt to deal with love in the first part and death in the second, but he has failed rather pitifully to organize the work either thematically or chronologically; the result is a meandering and redundant collection of reflections.

"She whose pure life was of my life a part" blessed him with a love in which there was "might," "majesty," and "greatness":

> Earth, like a joyous maiden whose pure soul
> Is filled with sudden ecstacy, became
> A fruitful Eden; and the golden bowl
> That held their elixir of life was filled
> To overflowing with the rarest draught
> Ever by gods or men in rapture quaffed.

In their happiness, they dreamed such dreams of love as "soften stern reality" and create an illusion of peace and harmony on earth:

A beautiful land is the Land of Dreams,
  Green hills and valleys and deep lagoons,
Swift-rushing torrents and gentle streams,
  Glassing a myriad silver moons.

But reality, in its sternest form, came to steal his child-wife away, leaving him to brood alone in her quiet room:

He sat again within the quiet room,
Where Death had snapped one golden thread of life,
And the pale hand of Sickness, sorrow-rife,
Robbed the plump cheek of childhood of its bloom.

Hope was gone; only sorrow and loneliness remained:

Oh, sorrow beyond all sorrows
  To which human life is prone:
Without thee, through all the morrows,
  To wander alone—alone!
Oh, dark, deserted dwelling!
  Where Hope like a lamb was slain,
No voice from thy love walls welling,
  No light in thy window pane.

Sangster was always able to find solace in his religious faith. He did not succumb dejectedly to sorrow but rather "looked far beyond for the celestial gain." He was prepared to give whatever God might ask because he believed that "They do not truly love who cannot yield/The mortal up to the immortal call." He was comforted too by the thought (which we have observed him to utter before) that man must be perfected through suffering.

"Into the Silent Land" is of no literary significance. It is unorganized and tautological, and some of its passages are painfully obscure. The verse is mechanical, and the language is forced. Even "Bertram and Lorenzo," which must qualify as one of the dullest poems ever published in Canada, is relieved by touches of color (and unintended humor), but "Into the Silent Land" is quite unrelieved from beginning to end either by freshness of image or felicity of phrase. Sangster's desire to avoid sentimentality is commendable, but he loses his poetic voice in the folds of his solemn garment of mourning, and emotion is not recollected in his lines. The London *Saturday Analyst and Leader* could not have been further off the mark in describing this collection of verse as "tenderly pathetic" and more worthy of attention than anything else in *Hesperus*.

V *Nature Poems*

We saw that nature was Sangster's main theme in the Orillia Woods sonnets and that some of his best nature description is to be found in "The Happy Harvesters." Of the other poems in which the nature theme is prominent, "The Falls of the Chaudiere" is the most ambitious. It opens impressively, with two of Sangster's most memorable lines: "I have laid my cheek to Nature's, placed my puny hand in hers,/Felt a kindred spirit warming all the life-blood of my face." But, unfortunately, the poem does not live up to the promise of its opening lines. It is a rambling, didactic piece of work on the well-worn subject of nature as the teacher of God's mysteries, and it is often proselytizing in tone. Unmindful of the words of welcome with which he greeted the iron horse to the idyllic world of "A Morning in Summer," Sangster describes man as the corrupter of the earth:

> God made the ancient hills,
> The valleys and the solemn wilderness,
> The merry-hearted and melodious rills,
> And strung with diamond dews the pine-trees' tresses;
>
> But man's hand built the palace,
> And he that reigns therein is simply man;
> Man turns God's gifts to poison in the chalice
> That brimmed with nectar in the primal plan. . . .

The poem contains many inept lines and such ludicrous phrases as "preacher-seas." The rhythm of the lengthy opening and concluding portions was borrowed, as Desmond Pacey points out, from Tennyson's "Locksley Hall"—obviously one of Sangster's favorite poems.

"One of his poems," wrote T. G. Marquis, in 1913, "has had a wider acceptance than any other by a Canadian poet. His stirring lyric on 'The Rapid' is a vivid, rousing bit of work. In language and rhythm it is splendidly imitative of the rush and sweep of the tumbling, leaping stretch of water so characteristic of Canadian streams."[2] Over the years, "The Rapid" has been more widely reproduced in texts and anthologies than any other of Sangster's poems, and it remains one of the few by which he is known to the poetry-reading public. Some commentators, however, have dismissed it out of hand as an imitation of Thomas Moore's "Canadian Boat Song" ("Faintly as tolls the evening chime. . ."). Probably Sangster did get the idea for his poem from Moore, but his poem is not a timid imitation. It is lighter in spirit than the "Canadian Boat Song," and its total onomatopoetic effect is better:

[98]

> All peacefully gliding,
> The waters dividing,
> The indolent batteau moved slowly along,
> The rowers, light-hearted,
> From sorrow long parted,
> Beguiled the dull moments with laughter and song:
> "Hurrah for the Rapid! that merrily, merrily
> Gambols and leaps on its tortuous way;
> Soon we will enter it, cheerily, cheerily,
> Pleased with its freshness, and wet with its spray."

Perhaps it was not, as E. K. Brown said, to write poetry of this sort that Sangster came into the world; but he did, while passing through, do a better job with verse of this sort than is sometimes allowed. Another good song of this type, which the Glasgow *Commonwealth* singled out for praise in its review of *Hesperus*, is "The Snows, Upper Ottawa."

Most of the other nature poems and lyrics in *Hesperus* are insignificant. "The April Snow Storm, April 1858" and "The Comet, October 1858" are both strained pieces of occasional verse. "Night and Morning" is a slight poem in ballad meter about a shipwreck. "A Thought for Spring," "The Swallows," and "Flowers" ("Thank God I love the flowers!") are all failures. "The Wren" is a silly little verse about the nature world of childhood:

> Each early spring the little wren
>   Came scolding to his nest of moss;
> We knew him by his peevish cry,
>   He always sung so very cross.
> His quiet little mate would lay
> Her eggs in peace, and think all day.

VI *Love Poems*

The most impressive shorter poem in this volume is "Lost and Found." Too slight a poem to be called an idyl, it is nevertheless idyllic. The significance of the title is that a shepherd boy who becomes lost in the hills happily finds a milkmaid and falls in love with her:

> In the mildest, greenest grove
>   Blest by sprite or fairy,
> Where the melting echoes rove,
>   Voices sweet and airy;
>   Where the streams
>   Drink the beams

Of the sun
As they run. . . .

Love is described in what may be the best four lines in Sangster:

Love is swift as hawk or hind
Chamois-like in fleetness,
None are lost that love can find
Sang the maid, with sweetness.

There was little in *The St. Lawrence and the Saguenay* to suggest that Sangster would be capable of such delicacy and assurance as he displays in this charming, almost-perfect little poem.

Some of the love lyrics in more conventional style are almost as delightful. In the first stanza of "Good Night," for example, Sangster is no longer merely talking about love, but conveying something of its magic:

We never say "Good Night,"
For our eager lips are fleeter
Than the tongue, the kiss is sweeter
Than parting words,
That cut like swords;
So we always kiss Good Night.

Unfortunately, he is unable to sustain the magic spell throughout the four stanzas of the poem. In the final stanza, we discover that "We've kissed our last Good Night," which largely spoils the effect. It is interesting to note that E. K. Brown cites this as one of Sangster's best poems. "True Love," in which Burns's influence can be sensed, and "Love While You May," a song in the manner of Thomas Moore, which R. P. Baker thinks has "all the glad paganism of Herrick's lyrics," are equally successful overall but are not up to the level of the opening stanza of "Good Night."

Another good lyric is "Young Again," which has a pleasant musical refrain. Less successful are "Gertrude" and "Love and Truth," which are marred by pomposity and moralizing. "Rose" is sprightly, at least, but rather glib:

Have a care, my merry maiden!
Young Adonis though he be,
Many hearts are secret-laden
That have trusted such as he.
Has he worth, and is he truthful?
Thoughtless maiden rarely knows;

> But, "He's handsome, brave, and youthful,"
> Says the heart of little Rose.

In "Crowned" and "Within Thine Eyes" the subject of love is approached more seriously. Finally, at the other end of the scale, is the happy, humorous song entitled "Clara and I," which even bad grammar does not spoil:

> We have a joke whenever we meet,
>   Clara and I;
> Prattle and laughter, and kisses sweet,
>   Clara and I.
> Were I but twenty, and not two score,
> Clara and I would laugh still more,
> With plenty of hopeful years in store
> For Clara and I, Clara and I;
> With plenty of hopeful years in store
>   For Clara and I.

Generally speaking, we find in this group of love poems a welcome simplicity and spontaneity. Sangster seems to have realized that he was incapable of high seriousness on the subject, and he has given his talents over almost exclusively in *Hesperus* to the lighter lyric. Most of the poems in this group would rank with his best work.

VII *Patriotic Poems*

In *The St. Lawrence and the Saguenay* there was only one poem on the subject of Canadian national pride; in *Hesperus* there are four. Before we discuss these, let us consider briefly the two poems welcoming Prince Arthur to Canada: "A Royal Welcome" and "England's Hope and England's Heir." "The lyrics welcoming the Prince of Wales are right hearty compositions," said the London *Saturday Analyst and Leader*, and the Glasgow *Commonwealth* stated that " 'England's Hope and England's Heir' quite redeems a twaddling class of ballatries, remarkable for little else, with but few rare exceptions, save fulsome adulation and false prediction." Sangster's pieces, it must be objected, do not really rise above the "twaddling class of ballatries," and they are plenty fulsome in their adulation for twentieth-century ears, but it is interesting to notice that even in these Empire pieces Sangster devotes much of his space to praising Canada:

> Welcome to our woodland deeps,
> To our inland lakes, and rivers,

Where the rapid roars and sweeps,
　　Where the brightest sunlight quivers.
Loyal souls can never fail;
　　Serfdom crouches in its lair;
But our British hearts are hale,
　　England's Hope and England's Heir.

"Song For Canada" is a martial song, "too full of fight for members of peace societies," E. H. Dewart said. In this song, Sangster praises the lakes, fields, and forests of Canada, the rural peace, the rustic toil, and the smiling, happy people. The "fight" is in the stirring chorus:

Let but the rash intruder dare
To touch our darling strand,
　　The martial fires
　　That thrilled our sires
Would flame throughout the land.

It is not clear which "rash intruder" Sangster had in mind, if any in particular. Relations with the United States were often strained, but the 1850's were quiet times in comparison with the 1860's.

In "The Plains of Abraham," another of the more widely anthologized of the poems, Sangster returns to the most dramatic of all Canadian historical events: Wolfe's defeat of Montcalm at Quebec in 1759 and the fall of both heroes on the field of battle. E. H. Dewart described this poem as "one of the most justly popular of our poet's pieces. . . . in which historic interest and martial spirit are felicitously blended." Its popularity cannot be justified on literary grounds. The poem is badly structured, and the diction is inflated. Neither is the martial spirit dominant, as Dewart suggests; the last stanza is devoted to deploring all wars, past and present. The following lines are as good as any in this lengthy poem:

I saw two great chiefs die,
Their last breaths like the sigh
Of the zephyr-sprite that wantons on the rosy lips of morn;
　　No envy-poisoned darts,
　　No rancour, in their hearts,
To unfit them for their triumph over death's impending scorn.

Desmond Pacey thinks that this is "the sort of product that almost any intelligent schoolboy might turn out if assigned the topic for a class exercise." There is a similar poem entitled "The Death of Wolfe," which the Kingston *News* thought "worthy of a high place in the esteem of every Anglo-Canadian," but it has even less literary merit.

The most interesting patriotic poem in *Hesperus* and the best one that Sangster ever wrote is "Brock," which he was commissioned to write for the unveiling of the new monument to Sir Isaac Brock at Queenston Heights on October 13, 1859, the original monument having been defaced by rebel sympathizers in 1837. Here is the complete poem:

> One voice, one people, one in heart
>> And soul, and feeling and desire!
>> Re-light the smouldering martial fire,
>> Sound the mute trumpet, strike the lyre,
>> The hero deed can not expire,
>>> The dead still play their part.
>
> Rise high the monumental stone!
>> A nation's fealty is theirs,
>> And we are the rejoicing heirs,
>> The honored sons of sires whose cares
>> We take upon us unawares,
>>> As freely as our own.
>
> We boast not of the victory,
>> But render homage, deep and just,
>> To his—to their—immortal dust,
>> Who proved so worthy of their trust
>> No lofty pile nor sculptured bust
>>> Can herald their degree.
>
> No tongue need blazon forth their fame—
>> The cheers that stir the sacred hill
>> Are but mere promptings of the will
>> That conquered then, that conquers still:
>> And generations yet shall thrill
>>> At Brock's remembered name.
>
> Some souls are the Hesperides
>> Heaven sends to guard the golden age,
>> Illuming the historic page
>> With records of their pilgrimage;
>> True Martyr, Hero, Poet, Sage:
>>> And he was one of these.
>
> Each in his lofty sphere sublime
>> Sits crowned above the common throng,

Wrestling with some Pythonic wrong,
In prayer, in thunder, thought, or song;
Briareus-limbed, they sweep along,
   The Typhons of the time.

There is little agreement among commentators on the literary merit of "Brock." The earlier commentators usually judged this and other of the martial pieces to be the best of Sangster's work. E. H. Dewart, for example, had high praise for these poems. R. P. Baker (1920) said that the poem "is full of passionate enthusiasm for the ideal of a united people," which was not really to assess its literary value. J. D. Logan and D. G. French (1924) described it as "a really noble hymn to the memory of a national hero," which was to say little more. E. K. Brown (1943) said that "this is Sangster when he has put on his formal singing robes: a little awkward, bent on doing his very best, and coming out of the ordeal with honour." Desmond Pacey, who is obviously not enamored of Sangster's patriotic verse, says that it "consists largely of platitudes uttered in a loud voice." Maybe patriotic verse demands platitudes. The poem is energetic and definitive in its pronouncements, which are the most important qualities of verse which would marshal patriotic sentiment. There is a slackening of tempo in the second, third, and fourth stanzas, but this helps to make way for the emotion to rise to a crescendo at the end. A. J. M. Smith's assessment seems like a fair one. "The last two stanzas," he says, "have a tortuous grandeur that redeems what otherwise would be merely conventional." Sangster's claim to a modest measure of fame as a patriotic poet rests largely on "Brock."

VIII *Miscellany*

In its review of *Hesperus*, the Glasgow *Commonwealth* singled out "My Prayer" as a "very beautiful devotional lay," and justly so. A number of other commentators have also called attention to it. A. S. Bourinot described it as "the purest poetry in the book," and H. Pearson Gundy says that in "simplicity, humility, and supplication before God" the poem "can rank with the well-known hymns of Cowper and Whittier."[3] The poem has thirteen stanzas, not all of which are of equal merit, but here are the two introductory stanzas in which, as Reverend Mr. Dewart might have said, Sangster's simple religious faith and lyrical facility are felicitously united:

O God! forgive the erring thought,
   The erring word and deed,

> And in thy mercy hear the Christ
> Who comes to intercede.
>
> My sins, like mountain-weights of lead,
> Weigh heavy on my soul;
> I'm bruised and broken in this strife,
> But Thou canst make me whole.

Although none of them is as pure as "My Prayer," "The Mystery," "The Unattainable," and "Her Star" are also successful hymnlike pieces.

"Grandpere" is a simple narrative poem which reflects, as R. P. Baker accurately observes, "the melody, the commonplaceness, and the sentimentality of Longfellow." Grandpere, age ninety-three, dies with his granddaughter, fair Eleanor, on his knee:

> He folded his arms around her,
> Like Winter embracing Spring;
> And the angels looked down from heaven,
> And smiled on their slumbering.

This is the only poem of its type in *Hesperus*, and even though it is sentimental, it is not unpleasant. The volume is also notably free from the more obnoxious forms of didacticism which characterized so much of the verse in *The St. Lawrence and the Saguenay*. "Glimpses," a poem in praise of honest toil, is bombastic, but the only really offensive piece in this respect is "Ingratitude," in which the drunkard is again the villain. Here is the second stanza, with its incredible opening line:

> Full on yon man-brute smiles the wife,
> To gladden his turbid breast;
> Savagely stern he seeks the life
> Where he erewhile sought for zest;
> With a curse, or worse, he ends the strife,
> And sinks to his drunken rest.

In contrast with this sort of thing, there is, finally, a fragile song of fantasy entitled "I'd Be a Fairy King," which has a happy, dancing rhythm and the quaint charm of such poems as "Mariline" and "Lost and Found":

> I'd be a Fairy King,
> With my vassals brave and bold;
> We'd hunt all day

Through the wildwood gay,
In our guise of green and gold.

This poem and several of the prayerlike poems in this volume belong with
Sangster's best work.

IX *Conclusion*

Ever since *Hesperus* was published in 1860, critical opinion has been
unanimous in rating it much above *The St. Lawrence and the Saguenay*.
What are the essential differences between the two volumes? The nature
theme, which is also religious, is dominant in both. There are fewer
religious nature poems in *Hesperus*, but then there are more purely
religious poems, such as "My Prayer." The love theme is no more prominent in one volume than in the other, in spite of claims to the contrary.
The theme of nationalism, implicit in *The St. Lawrence and the Saguenay*,
becomes explicit in *Hesperus*, but the significance of this has been exagger-
ated. Actually, "Brock" is the only patriotic poem for which a precedent
cannot be found in the first volume. Neither is there any marked increase
in Canadian subject matter in *Hesperus*, although this is often alleged.
Maple trees, Hurons, and other recognizably or distinctively Canadian
phenomena are more widely dispersed throughout *Hesperus*, to be sure,
but it takes all of them to add up to a bulk of Canadianness equivalent to
that of the title poem in the first volume. These are quantitative, rather
than qualitative considerations in any case, but they are points aften raised
in comparisons of the volumes. We must, however, look beyond themes
and subject matter for significant differences.

When we compare the poems in the two books in terms of types, stanza
forms, and verse forms, we do see some important differences. Realizing,
no doubt, that he was quite devoid of the sense of architectonics essential
for the successful structuring of a poem of the magnitude of "The St.
Lawrence and the Saguenay," Sangster did not attempt another one. There
are evident parallels between "The St. Lawrence and the Saguenay" and
the Orillia Woods sonnet sequence, but the structural demands of the
sequence, being much less stringent than those of the narrative, he produced a much better piece of work. His inability to unify a work of any
length or complexity can be clearly seen in the sequence too; he did not
overcome the problem; he simply strove to avoid it. Neither, of course, is
the sonnet form—at least not the free form which he uses—as demanding as
the Spenserian stanza, with which he experienced serious technical difficulties. He probably felt obligated to honor custom by writing a major

title poem for *Hesperus*, and personally obligated to produce a substantial piece of work in memory of his first wife. Otherwise, he wisely decided to write shorter and simpler poems for the second volume, using the conventional forms which had served him best and abandoning those which he could not master. In a sense, *Hesperus* is a triumph of critical judgment. Poems such as "Mariline," "The Happy Harvesters," and "Lost and Found" do represent departures though, both in form and technique. There is a happier marriage of form and content in these poems than in almost any other of the poems in either volume. The very artificiality of the heroic couplet, for example, which Sangster uses in "The Happy Harvesters," suits the artificiality of the subject matter perfectly and leads us to wonder if he might not have found his true voice in this verse form.

There are important stylistic differences too. The chastening was most obvious in the title poem in the second volume (where it was carried too far), but in general the writing is more highly polished. He has paid much more attention to technical detail, and the diction, although still quite literary, is only seldom incongruous. And he strictly curbed his sentimental and didactic tendencies. Perhaps the latter was as much a matter of good editing as anything else and may explain in part why the poems are shorter in general and why there are fewer of them in all. Edited out of the volume entirely, for example, were trite occasional verses, such as appeared in *The St. Lawrence and the Saguenay*, and introspective poems of a more subjective type.

There is really very little evidence in *Hesperus* of the development of greater poetic power, strictly speaking. The book represents, rather, a well-planned exploitation of strengths already demonstrated. The improved quality of the volume as a whole can be attributed almost entirely to more conscientious labor. Even poems such as "Mariline" and "The Happy Harvesters" are more noteworthy for their prettiness than for the evidence which they exhibit (although they do exhibit some) of new poetic strength. Sangster still has but little control over his talent, and inspiration comes to him only in spurts, but the inspired passages in *Hesperus* are not so frequently spoiled by banality in the next line as those in the first volume are. The next line is more likely to be competently written, even if it is unpoetic. Sangster stated the case for *Hesperus* reasonably well himself. The book displayed, he thought, "a more careful finish, more art, and a higher degree of mentality."

CHAPTER 6

The Unpublished Poetry

I The McGill Collection

We have already learned that Sangster's literary hopes and plans did not die with the publication of *Hesperus* in 1860 but remained with him until the end of his life. It is clear from his own statements in his letters and in notes in the manuscripts that most of his unpublished poems were written prior to, or during, the 1860's—before he joined the civil service. During the weary years of frustration and illness in Ottawa, his publishing plans remained nebulous. Until 1888, when he finally salvaged the time and energy to put his manuscripts in order, he had been thinking in terms of one new volume and a revised edition of *The St. Lawrence and the Saguenay*, from which he would exclude the many pieces which he found offensive and add instead a number of previously unpublished poems.

The title poem for *The St. Lawrence and the Saguenay* was revised and greatly expanded, as Sangster described in his letter of July 8, 1888, to W. D. Lighthall: "The leading poem in my first volume has been thoroughly re-written, and is twice as long as the poem in the first edition of the first volume, with notes, historical touches, etc. besides the Rapids—all in fact has been thoroughly re-written. In the first draft the Rapids are all compressed in one stanza—in the re-written edition they are all dealt with separately, giving to each a distinctive character of its own, and generally making the poem more complete, and more worthy of the subject." For a while, Sangster had rather special hopes for this book-length poem. A nephew, Amos W. Sangster,[1] a painter and engraver in Buffalo, New York, decided to issue an illustrated work on the Saint Lawrence and Saguenay rivers using his uncle's poem as the text. Sangster described this plan in his letter of November 15, 1888, to Lighthall: "My nephew, Amos W. Sangster, who is bringing his book on Niagara to a close, intends issuing another on the St. Lawrence and the Saguenay next year—that is, he expects to go down in the spring of 1889 to make sketches for the opening numbers. We will go down together, calling at Montreal, Quebec, and other places, taking in the Saguenay as far as Ha! Ha! Bay. . . . It is expected to take at least two years to complete, etching being very slow and tedious work. . . .

[108]

We will bring the MS with us and Amos W. will sketch from the text as we go along." Sangster sent the title poem to his nephew in 1889, but the latter became ill, and the plan was never realized. In his July 14, 1891, letter to Lighthall, Sangster said: "With respect to the leading poem in the book, it is locked up safely in my nephew's safe. . . . The contemplated trip he and I intended to make can I think never take place, although he hopes that it will."

Meanwhile, distinct from the scheme for the illustrated version of the revised title poem from *The St. Lawrence and the Saguenay*, Sangster's plans for the bulk of his unpublished work were taking shape. We return to his letter of November 15, 1888, to Lighthall: "In looking this MS over I find there is about—well between three and four thousand lines, very much in need of a publisher, and I must get this mass off my hands before I can do aught with the second editions of the other two volumes. This all done I am willing to turn my face to the wall and give up the ghost as soon as possible. There is too much for one volume, so I think of dividing it into two and selling it to the highest bidder. Then, if I live . . . turn my attention to *The St. Lawrence* and *Hesperus*, if my strength permits." It will be noticed that he planned, in addition to the illustrated volume which was never realized, a revised edition of *The St. Lawrence and the Saguenay*, which was, of course, to include the revised title poem. He revealed his thinking in detail in his letter of March 12, 1889, to Lighthall, from which we also get some idea of the anguish which attended his efforts:

Not only had I to defer a reply until now but to cease copying from my MSS the new volume I was preparing (two volumes in fact). A sudden attack of rheumatism in my right arm compelled me to desist. I am endeavouring to fight back the enemy, but I suppose that warmer weather must come, and the snow and moisture leave, before I can dislodge him. All I can do is to patiently await the result of my endeavours to gain the victory. Then I will go on with copying until the second volume is complete. After that I will have to copy the remainder of my MSS which will make a fourth volume about the size of *Hesperus*. I can do nothing with volumes one and two until all this is done. The slashing and passing through the crucible is pretty much done already. There will when all this is complete be four volumes, viz:

1. *The St. Lawrence & the Saguenay and Other Poems*
2. *Hesperus, etc.*
3. *Norland Echoes & Other Strains*
4. *The Angel Guest & Other Poems*

You see there will be a good deal of work for me to do, and I must not be in a hurry.

As we learned in Chapter 3, Sangster, fearing collapse at any time, mailed all of his manuscripts to Lighthall in the summer of 1891. He explained this action in his letter to Lighthall of July 14, 1891: "When I concluded to send you the MSS my idea was to save them, not to the world, but to this Canada of ours, which, as you know, has occupied my thoughts in the rhyming way for many years. I knew that you were inclined to harp a similar strain at times, and that begot a fellow feeling, which urged me on to make you a kind of literary executor, as it were—or rather yourself and John Reade. . . . I did not send them with a view to publication in the near future, but for safety, and for fear of my suddenly collapsing as other people were doing without warning. They occupied my thoughts incessantly, so that I made them up in two small volumes and sent them on, believing it to be the very best thing I could do." In spite of these statements, it was obviously Sangster's hope that Lighthall and Reade (the nucleus of the Society of Canadian Literature of Montreal) would find occasion to publish the manuscript poems in the not-too-distant future. Unfortunately, we do not have Lighthall's letters to Sangster, but it would seem to be clear from Sangster's letters that Lighthall expressed skepticism about the possibility of having the poems published, and it might realistically be supposed that he did not make any serious attempt to have them published. By 1899, the collection had already been deposited at McGill where, as we learned in Chapter 3, it lay unmolested for more than half a century.[2]

The manuscript poems are in seven rolls (ruled foolscap notebooks), and there are also a few poems and fragments scattered among the letters and other papers. Two of the rolls contain the corrected draft of *The St. Lawrence and the Saguenay*, with the notable exception of the revised title poem, which the poet sent to his nephew in Buffalo. The other five rolls contain the poems intended for the two entirely new volumes. Apparently, Sangster never completed his planned revision of *Hesperus*.

Each of the proposed new volumes was to have a measure of thematic integrity. *Norland Echoes*, as the title suggests, was to contain quite a number of poems on Canadian themes; *The Angel Guest* was to be composed largely of poems on religious and philosophical themes. However, each of the volumes was to have a sizeable section of "other" poems. Discounting the revisions, there are ninety-three poems in the McGill Collection. There are about fifty-eight lighter lyrics and songs, several odelike poems, some occasional verses, the "Midnight" sonnets which were introduced in Chapter 3, and a few narratives.

II *Canadian Poems*

The most interesting fact about the manuscript poems is that nearly a third of them have patriotic or nationalistic themes. While, as in the published volumes, there are several poems in which Sangster proclaims his loyalty to Queen and Empire, the majority of the poems are specifically Canadian in subject matter. There is no contradiction in Sangster's being both an upholder of the imperialist ideal and a Canadian nationalist. Part of Canada's greatness, in his eyes, is in the very fact that she shares in a civilization which girdles the globe.

Among the imperialistic poems are two platitudinous tributes to the monarchy and several lengthy narratives. "With the Iron Duke," a two-part poem of some three hundred and fifty lines on the subject of Wellington's campaign against the Napoleonic armies in Spain in 1811, belonged to the period of *The St. Lawrence and the Saguenay*, and Sangster planned to include it in the revised edition of that volume. The second and principal part of the poem is a narrative about the indecisive Battle of Fuentes de Onoro. The verse is energetic, but otherwise the poem is undistinguished. In 1861, the British ship *Trent*, which was carrying Confederate commissioners to Britain and France, was boarded on the high seas by the Americans, who seized the commissioners and returned them to Boston. The incident brought Britain and the United States to the brink of war, and it had the only somewhat less unfortunate effect of provoking Sangster to write his lengthy poem entitled "The War Cloud"—a narrative in limpid heroic couplets, with six lyrical interludes. The mood of the poem is almost impudently militant—the British flag has been insulted—but it ends, typically, with a "Hymn of Peace."

There are a number of military and marching songs in the manuscripts, of which "Bravo Volunteers," for which music was arranged by John C. Bonner of the Princess Louise Guards, Ottawa, to the tune of "Scots Wha Hae," is perhaps the best. Here is the first stanza:

> See, the border ruffians swarm,
> See, our brave defenders arm,
>   Bravo, Volunteers!
> Striplings rise like men today,
> Ripe for deeds that live for aye,
> Battle-brunt or lively fray,
>   Bravo, Volunteers!

A similar piece is "Marching Out Song," which was written for A. W. Murdoch for incorporation with a march which he did not live to complete.

A more explicitly nationalistic song is "God Bless the Dominion," which, Sangster says in an appended note, was written for the published music of a Mr. Sefton, a Toronto music teacher. "The Americans stole the air," says Sangster, "for the Star Spangled Banner." It would seem that Mr. Sefton was the real thief, however, since the tune, sung to words beginning "To Anacreon in Heaven . . . ," dates back to the London Anacreontic Society in the 1770's and was published in England in 1799. In any case, national patriotic songs are not usually notable for literary excellence, and Sangster's is not exceptional in this respect. Here is the first stanza:

> Dear land of my birth, there is no spot on Earth
>   We would choose before thee, with the wide world before us;
> O'er thy green hills and plains birdlike liberty reigns,
>   With the flag of the free floating royally o'er us.
>   True sons let us be of that race o'er the sea,
>   From whose loins we have sprung, whose ally we shall be,
>   While in heaven we trust, with one voice let us pray
>   God bless the Dominion for ever and aye.

And here is the introductory stanza of "Words For an Anthem" (published in *Belford's Monthly Magazine*, December, 1876), which is much the same:

> O, Power Supreme! in whose hands are the Nations,
>   Whose smile is the sun that illumines their way;
> Whose frown spreads a tremor through all the Creations
>   That move in the light of thy Sovereign sway;
>   Unite us as one, in this dawn of our glory,
>   That heralds a future no mortal can see,
>   When kingdoms and climes shall be proud of the story
>   Of Canada, Canada, Land of the Free.

"Jack, to the Nova Scotians" is a delightfully robust cheer for Confederation. Sangster displays greater spontaneity, originality, and humor in this attack on Joseph Howe's Nova Scotian resistance movement than we usually imagine him capable of, although the song's diction was influenced to some extent by Charles Dibdin's "Poor Jack." There are five stanzas and a chorus in all:

> Avast, ye lubbers! Clear the way,
> > Our stately ship's in motion—
> *The New Dominion*, decked as gay
> > As any craft on ocean.
> Sheet home the sails, run up the flag,
> > Who cares for Howe's opinion?
> Up goes the sail—in calm or gale
> > God bless the new Dominion!

Chorus

> > Then, trim your sails, run up the flag,
> > *A fig for Howe's opinion!*
> > *And from each lip the prayer let slip:*
> > *"God bless the New Dominion!"*

> And if a bluff old salt like Howe
> > Sings annexation snatches,
> We'll clear a corner down below,
> > And clap him under hatches.
> For we'll have none but British tars,
> > With British hearts to lead them;
> Who talks of scars and family jars,
> > We'll send for if we need them.

In commemoration of Confederation Day itself Sangster wrote sixty-four pious lines entitled "July First 1867." In this grandiloquent poem, he envisions Canadians asking God's blessing on the new nation:

> From New Brunswick's sea-washed harbours
> > Rolls the prayerful wavelet on,
> Through the wilds and sunny arbours,
> > Of the far Saskatchewan.

Knowing of his feelings toward Howe, we might wonder whether or not his failure to mention Nova Scotia was deliberate.

"Our Norland" was, of course, to be the title poem of one of the proposed volumes. Instead, this twelve-stanza poem was published in booklet form—posthumously, if we can accept the penciled date [1896] on the only copy known to exist. The chapbook, which displays Christmas decorations, was issued by the Copp Clark Company, Toronto, and the sole copy is in the James Collection of Canadiana at Victoria College of the University of Toronto. The published text varies slightly from the manuscript version in the McGill Collection, but nothing is known about the circumstances of its publication. The poem is not significant from the literary standpoint, although it is a sort of profession of faith in Canada on Sangster's part. Canada, he says, has none of the fabled creatures which people the literatures of the old world, but in her woods are real creatures just as exotic, and she has her own splendidly varied geography. She has no knights or barons in her history, but she has a race "as bold and brave": the Indians. Let us take pride in Canada, he says, as she moves towards becoming a great and unified nation:

> Stand up, then, in thy youthful pride,
>   O Nation yet to be,
> And wed this great land to its bride,
>   The broad Atlantic sea;
> Fling out Britannia's flag above
>   Our heaven-born endeavor,
> One chain of waves—one chain of love,
>   Uniting us forever.

There are quite a number of occasional verses and poems of tribute in the manuscripts on Canadian themes, the most ambitious of which is "Ode," a two-hundred-line tribute to D'Arcy McGee—one of the most illustrious of the Fathers of Confederation—who was assassinated by a Fenian outside the door of his boarding house in Ottawa, on the night of April 7, 1868. Sangster's poem, unfortunately, is ruined by ridiculously inflated diction and the utter absence of inspiration. Less significant in intention and of no literary merit whatever are "Well Done Clan Campbell," a poem on the marriage of the Marquis of Lorne and Princess Louise, daughter of Queen Victoria, in 1871; "Red Mac," a tribute to Colonel MacVicar, a Scottish-Canadian who joined the American northern army and lost his life at the Battle of Chancellorsville; and "The Little Stranger at Rideau Hall," a piece of sentimental claptrap about the birth of Canada's first "princess." Two other occasional verses come off only slightly better: "Hurrah for Hanlan" and "Oarsmen of St. John." The latter, which was published in *Stewart's Literary Quarterly Magazine* (January, 1869), is a tribute to the four Saint John oarsmen who captured the world championship at the 1867 Paris Exhibition, eight days after Confederation Day.

"Sillery" is a historical poem about an Iroquois attack on the missionary settlement at Sillery, New France, in 1648. In the description of the peacefulness of the village before and after the attack, there are echoes from Herbert's lyrics. "Voltigeurs of Chateauguay" (published in *The*

Saturday Reader, November 18, 1865) is a narrative about the repulse of an American force of fifteen hundred men at Chateauguay, Lower Canada, on October 26, 1813, by four hundred and sixty British soldiers (mostly French Canadians) under Col. Charles de Salaberry. "Saint-Denis" is a poem about the strife in 1837 at Saint-Denis, Lower Canada, where the British force was defeated by a group of insurgents, who also captured and murdered British Lt. John Weir. In retaliation for Weir's murder, the British sacked and burned Saint-Denis. Sangster's poem, which probably dates from the period, is a diatribe against rebellious acts and a plea for peace and harmony in the land.

A much more ambitious poem is "The Rebel," which was mentioned briefly in Chapter 1. In a note in the manuscript, Sangster says that this poem was begun in 1839 and intended for a work in three cantos, but it was never finished and lay lost among his papers for fifty years. Two cantos exist, if we assume that the second one is complete, and the fragment is eight hundred lines in length. In the first canto, we are introduced to a forest homestead setting which breathes such a toxic aroma of mellow, pastoral romanticism that we have to keep reminding ourselves that we are supposed to be on a pioneer farm in the Canadian woods. Here reside an old man, with "reverential locks of snow," and his "fair daughter" and "brave son," though the latter, in truth, is a black (and rebellious) sheep. The second canto deals explicitly with the Rebellion of 1837:

> Through the forest, through the village,
> Treason reeled with blood and pillage;
> Knaves who feared to face the light,
> Prowled like wolf-packs through the night;
> Women, babes, and old men hoary,
> Victims fell to sack and foray.

Sangster makes no attempt to veil his contempt for the cause of 1837 or for Mackenzie, the rebel leader in Upper Canada, who fled to the United States to avoid capture:

> While his dupes lay dead or dying,
> He amongst the foremost—flying.
> Not so Nelson—rash but brave,
> Full of courage as of speech,
> Battling where he could not save,
> Fighting in the fiery breach.

But the Traitor who's a coward—
Let him rot! no friendly Howard
Putting forth an arm to free
His double crime from Infamy.

"The Rebel" is characteristic in many ways of Sangster's work. By the age of seventeen, he had already acquired his crippling poetic vocabulary and his habit of imitating the forms and phrases of other poets. He progressed beyond this in technique, but the die of his poetic future was cast by 1839.

"Tapooka," the first of four Indian poems, was published in Dewart's *Selections.* Tapooka had a Sioux brave lover, but custom dictated that she become the wife of the chief of a neighboring tribe. A great wedding feast was planned:

From the banks of the Cadaracqui,
From Niagara's solitudes,
Where the song of the Water Spirit
Rolled vast through the primal woods:

From Superior's rocky defiles,
Her grand and rugged shores,
From Ottawa and blue waved Erie
Came the Chiefs and the Sagamores.

But Tapooka would not resign herself to her fate; she fled to the forest and took her own life by leaping from a cliff, leaving only a legend behind:

At night when the stars are shining
And the moon with silvery hue
Illumins the lake with radiance,
Is seen a white canoe:

Two shadowy forms within it,
Two faces that seem to smile—
The maid and her brave Sioux lover,
Returned from the Spirit-Isle.

As we read this and other timidly imitative Indian poems, we cannot help but contrast them mentally with the crisp realism of D. C. Scott's treatment of similar themes, as, for example, in the following lines from "At Gull Lake: August, 1820":

> Twice the Chief fired at the tents
> And now when two bullets
> Whistled above the encampment
> He yelled "Drive this bitch to her master."

How prim and ineffectual Sangster is by comparison!

"The Iroquois," which was published in the *Canadian Monthly and National Review* (September, 1873), is a shameless imitation of Byron's "Destruction of Sennacherib":

> Dread scourge of the forest! Swift Angel of Death!
> The winds at thy coming paused, trembled for breath;
> And the stately Algonquin, long feared in the fight,
> Hurled his tribesmen in vain 'gainst the Iroquois might.

Byron's poem ends with the widows wailing; Sangster's, with the Iroquois whooping! "Tecumseh," which was also published in the *Canadian Monthly and National Review* (July, 1872), is a tribute to the memory of the Shawnee chief Tecumseh (1768–1813), who served as a brigadier general in charge of Indian troops in the British army in the War of 1812, and died in the Battle of Moraviantown. "The Red Man" is an uninspired, meditative poem of some hundred lines of blank verse on the mystery of the origin of the North American Indian.

It must be admitted that there is little that is new in this group of Canadian poems, but "Jack, to the Nova Scotians" and the anthems for Canada, in particular, provide surer evidence of the sincerity of Sangster's belief in Confederation and a Canadian nation than his published volumes do. He definitely came to regard himself as Canada's national poet.

III *Poems of Love*

Happily, in most of the love poems in the manuscripts, we find the more mature Sangster, emancipated from both the high seriousness of his earliest love poems and the imitativeness which persisted, even in *Hesperus*.

"Love the Little Cavalier" is not as fresh and dainty as "Lost and Found," but the same lighthearted spirit frolics through it. Here are all five stanzas:

> One merry morn in merry May,
> Young Love beneath the rose-bush lay;
> No rose upon the fragrant tree

Was half so fair a rose as he.
    "I droop, I pine in sadness here,"
    Sighed Love, the Little Cavalier.

No rose upon the fragrant tree
Was half so fair a rose as he.
The gardener's daughter, gentle Maud,
Tripped like a sunbeam o'er the sod;
    "A shining orb to grace my sphere! "
    Cried Love, the little Cavalier.

The gardener's daughter, gentle Maud,
Tripped like a sunbeam o'er the sod;
And from behind a flowering thorn
The young Earl stepped, as fresh as morn.
    "Another orb, as I'm a seer! "
    Laughed Love, the Little Cavalier.

And from behind the flowering thorn
The young Earl stepped as fresh as morn.
Maud's lily hand the young Earl took—
Could Love mistake the dual look?
    "Spirit of Truth, appear! appear! "
    Cried Love, the Little Cavalier.

Maud's lily hand the young Earl took—
Could Love mistake the dual look?
Home to their hearts with grateful joy,
They took the smiling, rosy boy:
    "Pray take me in without a fear,"
    Said Love, the Little Cavalier.

The simple diction and the clever use of incremental repetition give this poem a nursery-rhyme quality. It was published in *Belford's Monthly Magazine* (April, 1878).

The mischief of "Clara and I" finds a more satisfying expression in "Under the Hill," which is the most attractive poem of its type in Sangster. Here the love theme is handled with objectivity and admirable frugality. The diction is simple and appropriate; the rhythm is almost flawless; and the tone is right throughout:

        Under the hill,
       When the night winds are still,
   Alice is waiting quite close to the mill;

> Waiting, and thinking: "The time is so long!
> Would he were come, like the air to the Song;
> Long have I watched for him here at the mill,
> Far from my cottage there under the hill."

> Softly and bright,
> On the mellow June night,
> Golden and graceful the moon heaves in sight;
> "Somebody's coming now—this is the time—
> Now by the poplars—now, under the lime! "
> Quickly love's searching eye traces him still:
> By the brook—past the brook—*here*, at the mill.

> Up the hill,
> Statuesque-like and still,
> Shadows in silhouette fall on the mill:
> Rogueish-eyed Alice! On tiptoe she stands:
> Stoops the young miller and presses her hands—
> Presses her lips, too, yet all is so still—
> None but the moon sees them, under the hill.

The images evoked by the two hyphenated adjectives in the third stanza—
"statuesque-like" and "rogueish-eyed"—tell us more about Alice than
Sangster succeeded in conveying about his companion on the Saint Lawrence and the Saguenay in a hundred and ten stanzas, or in twenty-two
sonnets about a seeming host of fair companions in the Orillia Woods.

"Brown-Eyed Jane" has neither the vitality of "Love the Little Cavalier"
nor the sparkle of "Under the Hill," but it is characterized by the same
carefree approach to love as these poems are. Here are the first two
stanzas:

> Shall I sit by you my brown-eyed Jane?
> Make you a song while you're making flowers?
>   We'll not heed what the wise ones say—
>   Creatures who sift our human clay;
> I know you best who sit by you, Jane,
> Making a song while you're making flowers,
> And reading the light of your eyes for hours.

> You are no beauty, my brown-eyed Jane,
> Fashioned and moulded from finest soil;
>   Many a beauty, though, would give
>   Half of the life she's forced to live
> For the power that lies in your brown eyes, Jane,
> Beaming such light on your dainty toil.

This has the distinction of being the only poem in which Sangster carries his cultural primitivism to the point of depicting a maiden not fair to the view—a refreshing departure, which contributes to the poem's appeal.

In "Marion," the note of contempt for the privileged which was discreetly sounded in "Brown-Eyed Jane" becomes noisy didacticism:

> Shame, shame on my lady, cold of heart!
> Learn of the humblest to play your part,
> Learn of your maid to say ere long—
> Blessed be Marion's heart of song.

A more serious but more successful lyric than "Marion" is "Once Seen." More like Sangster's published love lyrics in diction and tone, the concluding lines of each of the three stanzas are especially noteworthy:

> Were I an angel, starred and crowned,
>   I'd cleave to the unresisting space,
> And search through all the steller round
>   To gaze upon her face.
> I'd hang with rapture on her words,
>   And quaff her looks as men quaff wine,
> Until my thoughts, like summer birds,
>   Made music for this love of mine.
>
> Fain would my spirit-searchings trace
>   Her soarings to the higher goal,
> And read in her beloved face
>   The secrets of her soul;
> What visions of seraphic life,
>   What virgin rapture, pure desire!
> Burning the dross of human strife
>   With scintils of celestial fire.
>
> Thus would I have her—good as fair,
>   And just the seraph that she seems;
> Her every thought and look a prayer,
>   Pervading all her dreams.
> I'd pluck the rosebuds of her words,
>   Learn the sweet language of her eyes,
> And all my hopes like summer birds,
>   Would sing in this new Paradise.

Had Sangster's literary ambitions and pretentions been more modest, he might have become an excellent song writer. Even without trying very hard (though he was a student of English song writers) he wrote more good songs than most other Canadian poets—hymns, martial songs, love songs, and children's songs. There are proportionately more songs in the manuscripts than in the published volumes, and it would seem as though a number of these were written during the Ottawa years. Quite a few of them were set to music or were written for existing music. Music for "Mabel," which has that anesthetic quality of a "good, old song," was composed by John C. Bonner, sometime bandmaster of the Princess Louise Guards, Ottawa:[3]

> I would I were the Fay that roams
>   Through some enchanted dell,
> I'd live on sips from Mabel's lips,
>   And soothe her with a spell;
> And hers should be such dreams, as ne'er
>   Were dreamt by mortal's brain,
> And time would fly, and years go by
>   Or ere she waked again.
>
> Through all the bounds of Faerie
>   I'd seek the wizard old,
> Whose magic skill would rear for me
>   A palace all of gold;
> Of gold and gems, and precious stones,
>   And Parian marbles fair;
> Of tinted walls and perfumed halls,
>   And wealth of jewels rare.
>
> A storm of airs from Fairyland
>   Love's pleading voice would seem,
> Whose witching strains would break the chains,
>   Of Mabel's happy dream;
> And she should wake to rank and state,
>   To see all Elfland throng
> To crown me Lord of all her realm,
>   And her my Queen of Song.

"Nellie of the Glen" was also set to music by John C. Bonner. This song is not as polished as "Mabel" is, and the first stanza is spoiled by the bathos of this line: "For love of fair Nellie the lads have grown thin." Sangster was capable of misplaced humor, and he sometimes faltered from a lack of a sense of it altogether.

For one reason or another the remaining love poems in the manuscripts are less successful than most of those quoted above. "Happy as a Birdie" is as sentimental as its title suggests it to be. "The Fishers," a mystical love poem, is a very feeble piece of work, but for some reason Sangster chose to let it appear in the *Canadian Monthly and National Review* (September, 1875). There are two poems with "gold-plated" rhythms—"Eva's Prayer" and "Not Found"—and in both cases the rhythms gallop away, oblivious to the words around them. For example, here are four lines from "Not Found," which has the rhythm of Thomas Moore's "To the Large and Beautiful Miss . . .":

> She is fair as the truth in a seraphic soul
> Or the hue of a delicate rose;
> Her eyes have the gleam of the planets that roll
> Like dreams through the midnight's repose.

Pleasant as it is to find that in this group of love lyrics Sangster is handling the love theme with assurance and originality, what is more striking is the poverty of the collection in terms both of scope and quality. "Love the Little Cavalier" and "Under the Hill" are among Sangster's best short poems, and several of the others make easy and pleasant enough reading, but beyond these there is little worth preserving.

IV Poems on Death

There were several undistinguished poems in *The St. Lawrence and the Saguenay* on the subject of death, and the section "Into the Silent Land" in *Hesperus* devoted to the memory of Mary Kilborn Sangster. As a Romantic, Sangster probably would have written on death and mourning irrespective of the circumstances of his personal existence, but when we recall that his twenty-two-year-old wife died in 1858, his mother in 1863, and his four-year-old daughter in 1868, it is not surprising to find a large number of poems about death in manuscripts which date from the very period of these unlucky events.

The major poem in this category is "The Angel Guest," the title poem for one of the unpublished volumes. The idea on which the poem is based is an altogether conventional one, which Sangster expressed several times in the published volumes: the human soul descends from heaven at birth and returns there at death. The incident is the death of a small child, and in Sangster's religio-mystical imagination the insubstantial narrative of the "angel guest" is woven from the religious premise and the sadness of the occasion. The narrative is supposed to provide the unifying thread, but once again—as in "The St. Lawrence and the Saguenay," "Hesperus," "Into the Silent Land," and the Orillia Woods sonnet sequence—Sangster's inability to structure a work of any length or complexity is obvious. The narrative is too frail to sustain a poem of nearly four hundred lines, and the transitions from one phase of the narrative to another could scarcely have been more ineptly handled. Again, the rhythm has been borrowed from Tennyson and, like "Hesperus," the poem is intended to be symphonic. In spite of the fact that there is usually more of cacophony than euphony, it does have a few rare moments of musical splendor.

The first eighteen stanzas tell of the sweet music made on harp and lyre by the angel child before her human birth. Following are the first, second, seventh, ninth, and eighteenth stanzas:

> In the land of the Immortals dwelt an
> > Angel Child, whose lyre
> Stirred the Souls with wild seraphic flashes
> > of melodious fire.

> Lyre and harp flung strains so perfect through
> > the hills that rose and fell,
> Shaking mists of purple perfume down
> > the heights of asphodel.

> All the stars through all their courses, speeding
> > through the astral way,
> Suns and moons and peopled planets,
> > joined in that Celestial lay.

> As the sunset floods the heavens with a golden-
> > crimson fire,
> So the wilds of space were flooded with the
> > sweetness of her lyre.

> And the days rolled by like moments
> > wafted through ambrosial air;
> Hers the sweetest harp in heaven,
> > hers the gentlest spirit there.

The next thirty-three stanzas tell of the earthward flight of the "angel guest" with a host of ten thousand heavenly spirits. The clumsiness of the first narrative transition is illustrated by the bathos of the nineteenth stanza:

> But the time has reached its fulness
> > when the Angel Child should go

> On a fine and holy mission
>> to two waiting hearts below.

And the fifty-second stanza, in which the "angel guest" enters the human world, is only slightly less distressing:

> Like a solemn benediction,
>> softer than the smiles of morn,
> Sped the cry through earth and heaven:
>> "Lo, another child is born! "

Twenty-four stanzas, many of which are tacky with sentimentality, are devoted to the angelic qualities of the newborn child. Here, for example, is stanza sixty-two:

> What were all the starry splendours
>> of the brightest wintry skies
> To the gleams we had of heaven
>> in the starbeams of her eyes?

Finally, the "angel guest" is recalled to heaven, and the earthly parents are left to grieve. This is stanza seventy-eight:

> All our hopes that soared so lark-like,
>> till they lost themselves in air,
> Fluttered down, maimed, wounded, bleeding,
>> through the night of our despair.

The poem is much too long, and it makes dull reading. There are some pleasantly melodious passages, but the borrowed rhythm haunts the ear. The diction is inflated, and there are many borrowed phrases—especially from Milton. In short, the poem displays most of Sangster's weaknesses and few of his virtues as a poet. It is an almost total failure.

The other poems about death and mourning are no better. "Lottie" is the title of a group of three sentimental lyrical tributes to Sangster's daughter Charlotte and is reminiscent of "The Little Shoes," which was published in Dewart's *Selections* in 1864. "Answered," an insignificant verse about the spirit of a dead child hovering over the grave, was published in *Belford's Monthly Magazine* (October, 1877) as "The Two Angels." "Another Child of Promise," an elegiac tribute for a child, is "inscribed to the bard Evan MacColl," and there are two similar poems of tribute: "C. J. B. 1841–1867" and "Walter Munro." The latter was published in *Belford's Monthly Magazine* (April, 1877), but none of these poems, nor several others not mentioned, are worthy of serious attention.

V *Miscellany*

Nature was the dominant theme of the published poetry, but it is not an important theme in the manuscript poems. In "Cowslips Were Blooming on the Hills," "Eugene," a "blue-eyed, fair-haired delight" of a man searches among "untrodden ways" for truth in nature. "Whispers of the Rills" echoes not only Wordsworth, but Coleridge, Keats, and Tennyson as well—but it may, nonetheless, be the best of these nature poems. Here are the first three of its twenty-seven quatrains:

> Weary with scrambling up the sides
>   So rugged of the Ardley hills,
> I strayed from my adventurous guide
>   To trace the rills
>
> That trickled down from rock to rock,
>   In merry glidings, falls and leaps,
> To where the Brook, with ruder shock,
>   Impulsive sweeps.
>
> Here over crags they skipped in turn,
>   Here skipping through a leafy arch,
> They kissed the bare roots, old and worn,
>   Of the mountain larch.

"Quinté" was published in the *British American Magazine* (May, 1863). It affords but little evidence of close observation, but it is pleasantly quiet:

> Spirit of Gentleness! what grace
> Attends thy footsteps. Here thy face
> With fine creative glory shone,
> Like a mild seraph's near the Throne,
> On that fair morn when first thy wing
> Passed o'er the water, brightening
> The quiet shores that gravely lay
> Far, far along the tranquil bay.

"Niagara" is much less successful, and so is "At the Chaudiere," which was published in the *Canadian Monthly and National Review* (March, 1872).

"Our Own Far North" is Sangster's only poem in praise of the north, but it is very weak.

There is no religious verse of any significance in the manuscripts, and the philosophical and introspective pieces are not really deserving of discussion, although Sangster had at least three of them published—"The Greater Sphinx" in *Stewart's Literary Quarterly Magazine* (October, 1868); and "Life" and "Asleep" in *Belford's Monthly Magazine* (March, 1877, and February, 1878, respectively). A few of the more subjective of these poems betray profound despair and bitterness. In "The Life Chase," Sangster sees life as a crooked game:

> But still we go searching, searching
> Through windings that have no end,
> While a cheat called life with pain is rife,
> With death for our only friend.

"Drifting" is more personal:

> My life is lost,
> Each fond hope crossed,
> And I, a lone bark, seaward tossed.
> But on, on, on,
> From dark to dawn,
> I'm wafted like a crippled swan.

Sangster is almost incredibly inarticulate in "The Interruption," a fifty-line poem of the most morbid sort, but these two lines are clear: "O sad life, and forlorn! /Better I had ne'er been born."

The lengthiest of the poems in the "philosophical" group is a formidable piece of writing entitled "The Reading." It is in eight parts and is more than four hundred lines in length. In a painfully labored blank-verse introduction, an undefined body of "friends," including a skeptical individual, hear one of their number eulogize a deceased poet friend. Then the dead poet's "love lay"—"The Universal Story"—a poem "besprent with lyrics," is read. The poet was a "hunter in men's thoughts and words" and a student of nature's laws. "The Universal Story" does have a few good lines, but generally speaking it is barren and directionless. By means of lyrical interludes (poems within a poem, within the poem), we are led through misty realms of Love, learning of its awakening: "Mounting up with glad surprise/To the watch-tower of her eyes." Of its youthful hopes: "Through her soul of childlike mien/Forms and voices Sybilline/Twine her hopes with evergreen." Of its loss and rediscovery: "And a calm voice overhead/Heard above the thunder, said:/"Love, though wounded, is not dead."" And then the poem ends as it began, in blank verse, with "the erstwhile doubter, his opinion changed," marveling at the poet's power to penetrate the mystery of Life.

Turning to the occasional verse, "Pam," which was published in the *Saturday Reader* (December 2, 1865), is a tribute to Lord Palmerston, prime minister of Great Britain. "Peabody" is a tribute to George Peabody, the American philanthropist and promoter of Anglo-American relations. "C. D." is a tribute to Charles Dickens. "C. D." and "Peabody" definitely date from Sangster's Ottawa years. "Bryant," the best of these occasional verses in spite of its grandiloquence, was written in 1864. The following lines from it are in praise of poets in general:

> All honour to the lyric few
>   Of every land and nation,
> The tuneful throng whose souls of song
>   Are deeps of inspiration:
> O sad old world, where were thy boast
>   Unless these struck the lyre?
> Thou hadst no mental Pentecost
>   But for their tongues of fire.

In terms of banality, a lengthy narrative entitled "The Russian Legend" is surpassed only by an even lengthier narrative entitled "The Double Surprise." The latter, which was intended as a humorous poem, is a complete failure. Happy to say, Sangster did leave one humorous (if very minor) poem in the manuscripts—"Sauney and Pat":

> Give me a Scot for common sense;
> I care not who, there's none more brave;
> He takes just one side of the fence,
> Nor straddles it to mouth and rave.
> He's leal and loyal to himself,
> Loyal to Britain, or, if not,
> No paltry bribe of place or pelf
> Will make him do a single jot.
> But my Irish friend across the stair,
> Who smokes my pipe and drives my mare,
> May be a jolly Fenian rare;
> While *he* o'erflows with loyal phrases
> He'd cut my throat from ear to ear,
> And send my British "soul" to blazes.

One of the best short poems in the manuscripts is "Rosy Dreams." In this poem, Sangster keeps sentimentality and nostalgia in check as, in easy numbers, with his poet's eye better focused than usual, he returns to "life's happier day":

> My heart is wandering back again
>   In rosy dreams today,
> As half in peace, and half in pain,
>   I while the hours away;
> I tread the fields with boyish feet,
>   I muse along the shore,
> And coloured meads as rare and sweet,
>   As in the days of yore.
>
> The black bird warbles in the hedge,
>   The cheery notes of spring,
> And in the blooming hawthorne hedge,
>   The robin comes to sing;
> The fisher-lights dart up and down,
>   Like will-o-wisps at play,
> And starbeams gleam across my dream,
>   As in life's happier day.
>
> The thrushes sing, the fair-haired boy
>   Within the garden delves,
> Where merry feet make music sweet
>   As tripping of the elves;
> The old house seems a palace, as
>   We tread the humble floor,
> And skies are blue, and hearts are true,
>   As in the days of yore.

A delightful song with something of the gusto of Bliss Carman's better "ballads" is "A Northern Rune," which was published in Dewart's *Selections* and reprinted in Campbell's *Oxford Book of Canadian Verse*. Here are the first stanza and the chorus, which were written to be sung to the tune of "The Brave Old Oak":

> Loud rolleth the rune, the martial rune,
>   Of the Norse-King-Harpist bold;
> He's proud of his line, he's erect as a pine
>   That springs on the mountains old.
> Through the hardy north, when his song goes forth
>   It rings like the clash of steel;

> Yet we have not a fear, for his heart's sincere,
> And his blasts we love to feel.

> *Chorus*   *Then hi for the storm!*
> *The wintry storm,*
> *That maketh the stars grow dim;*
> *Not a nerve shall quail,*
> *Not a heart shall fail,*
> *When he rolls his grand old hymn.*

Sangster regarded children so fondly that he found it difficult to write of them, or for them, without lapsing into sentimentality, but "Boy and Girl" is quite restrained:

> Tell me, my roving boy, were *you* a fly,
> Would you be off to the hills so high?
> Teasing the antelope, biting the deer,
> Stinging huge giants in castles drear?
> Or with the bee over flowery fields,
> Feed on the nectar and clover yields?

> Were I a fly I'd have none of these;
> With folded wings I'd sit at my ease,
> And leaving the mountains so far below
> They'd seem like pebbles, so high we'd go;
> Higher, and higher, and ever so high,
> I'd ride on my rocking horse up to the sky.

The best children's poem in the manuscripts is unquestionably "Little Jack Frost," which speaks for itself:

> Little Jack Frost went up the hill,
> Watching the stars so cold and chill,
> Watching the stars and the moon so bright,
> And laughing about like a crazy wight.

> Little Jack Frost ran down the hill,
> Late in the night when the winds were still,
> Late in the Fall, when the leaves fell down,
> Red and yellow, and faded brown.

> Little Jack Frost walked through the trees,
> "Ah," cried the flowers, "We freeze—we freeze! "

"Ah," sighed the grasses, "We die—we die! "
Said Little Jack Frost, "Goodbye, goodbye."

Little Jack Frost skipped round and round,
Spreading light snow on the frozen ground;
Nipping the breezes, icing the streams,
And chilling the warmth of the sun's bright beams.

Nobody saw him, still he was there,
Nose-biting, prank-playing everywhere;
All through the houses, out in the street,
Capering wildly through storm and sleet.

But when Dame Nature brought back the Spring,
Brought back the bird to chirp and sing,
Melted the snow and warmed the sky,
Little Jack Frost went pouting by.

The flowers opened their eyes of blue,
Green buds peeped out and grasses grew,
And it got so warm and scorched him so,
Little Jack Frost was glad to go.

VI *The New* St. Lawrence and the Saguenay

The revised edition of *The St. Lawrence and the Saguenay* was prepared shortly after the publication of *Hesperus*. In 1862, H. J. Morgan stated that the "leading poem in Mr. Sangster's first volume has recently been entirely re-written";[4] and in 1865, the *Saturday Reader* indicated that the revised edition of the first volume was soon to be published.[5] Both Morgan, in his *Sketches of Celebrated Canadians*, and the *Saturday Reader* published sample stanzas from the revised title poem, and these stanzas (eight in all) are now all that we have of the new title poem of over two hundred stanzas. The manuscript was last heard about in 1891, when Sangster claimed that it was secure in his nephew's safe in Buffalo, New York. It is to be doubted that it still exists. Amos W. Sangster died in Buffalo in 1903, willing his estate to a spinster niece. This Miss Sangster, who claimed to be "the last of the Sangsters," was a schoolteacher in Buffalo. When she died, she willed all of her possessions to a lady residing (until recently, at least) in Buffalo, who stated that she had never heard Miss Sangster mention either the manuscript or its author. The Erie County Historical Society has but a single Sangster letter, which Amos W. wrote to his sister Wrania, and the Buffalo and Erie County Public Library has no Sangster papers at all.[6]

The four new stanzas which Morgan quoted in his sketch are those in which the Saint Lawrence rapids are more fully treated than they were in the original. Sangster thought this a significant improvement, because he mentioned it twice in his letters to Lighthall, but it is only an expansion, written in even more inflated language than the original. He strives to convey the rapids' strength by comparing them with champions, autocrats, demons, titans, dragons, and so on; he does not describe what he actually observes. The following stanza on the Lachine rapid, at the conclusion of which he stoops to the sort of didacticism which characterized "Pity's Tear Drop," suggests that the loss of the manuscript of the revised title poem should not be regarded as a catastrophe:

> The waves of two vast streams fall down to thee,
> And worship at thy feet. The pilgrim bands
> In untold legions rush to bend the knee,
> All victims to the Dragon, that demands
> Its multitudes, as countless as the sands,
> And ope's its jaws for more. So Error keeps
> High jubilee through all earth's blessed lands,
> Above which evermore sweet Pity weeps,
> To see the blinded fools embracing death by leaps.

The six stanzas which were published in the *Saturday Reader* were numbers one hundred and thirty-four and following of the new version. The first two of the six are revisions of former stanzas; the other four are outright additions. The magnitude of the expansion can be appreciated from the fact that the forty-ninth stanza in the original poem became the one hundred and thirty-fourth stanza in the new version. A comparison of the original of the forty-ninth stanza with the revision provides a good picture of the character of Sangster's revisions. He pays strictest attention to faulty rhythm, but he also attempts to clarify vague lines and sweeten the diction:

> Th' inconstant moon has passed behind a cloud,
> *The changeful* moon has passed behind a cloud,
>
> Cape Diamond shows its sombre-colored bust,
> Cape Diamond *rears* its *high, gigantic* bust,
>
> As if the mournful night had thrown a shroud
> *Dimly*, as if the night had thrown a shroud
>
> Over this pillar to a hero's dust.
> *Upon it, mindful of* a hero's dust.

Well may she weep; hers is no trivial trust;
Well may she weep; hers is no *common* trust;

His cenotaph may crumble on the plain,
His *C*enotaph may crumble on the plain,

Here stands a pile that dares the rebel's lust
But this vast pile *defies* the *traitor's* lust

For spoilation: one that will remain—
For spoilation; *here his hate was vain*;

A granite seal—brave Wolfe! set upon Victory's Fane.
Nature, enraged, alone could rend the mass in twain.

Here is some improvement, certainly, but since neither the original nor the revision exhibits much evidence of poetic sensibility, the futility of it all strikes us more forcibly than does the pleasure of seeing some of the worst wrinkles ironed out of the lines. The revisions are mechanical, and the new stanzas are merely mechanical interpolations. The four additional stanzas on Wolfe add no more to the poem than do the additional stanzas on the rapids.

Sangster planned to omit about half of the "other poems," to add a few previously unpublished poems (such as the narrative about the Duke of Wellington), and to include a few poems essentially unchanged from the first edition and quite a number of revisions. Unfortunately, when it came to revisions, he usually expanded the poems, when deletions might have meant improvements. An example is his revision of "Canadian Sleigh Song"—one of the most unaffected pieces in the first volume. In this case, he spoiled the songlike appearance of the poem by lengthening the lines to make quatrains out of the octaves. He also thickened the diction, complicated the rhythm, and added a chorus. Here is the spontaneous first stanza of the original version followed by the first stanza of the revised version:

Tinkle, tinkle, tinkle,
Merrily, merrily, O,
Chime the tuneful sleigh bells,
Singing to the snow;
Tinkle, tinkle, tinkle,
Merrily, merrily, O,
Laughs the dimpled Maiden,
Chatting to her beau.

. . . .

> "Merrily sing, sweet love-thoughts, merrily, merrily, O,"
> Chime the silvery sleigh-bells, spangled with the snow;
> "Merrily sing, sweet love-birds, merrily, merrily, O,"
> Laughs the joyous-hearted maiden, chatting to her beau.
>
> *Chorus:*   *The storm may howl above us,*
> *Life's skies are all aglow,*
> *When we think of those that love us,*
> *And the blessings of the snow.*

At best, Sangster succeeded in effecting minor technical improvements through the process of revision. There is no example to be found of him having substantially strengthened a weak poem, and there is no evidence whatever of poetic insight having guided any of the alterations or additions.

VII *Conclusion*

Hesperus was almost too well written and too skillfully edited to fit into the picture which *The St. Lawrence and the Saguenay* gave us of Sangster. How, we might ask ourselves, could he have learned so much in such a short period of time? The unpublished poems make this question even more difficult to answer, because the lessons learned between 1856 and 1860 have not been applied to the manuscript volumes. In fact, the manuscript poems as a whole do not make up a collection as impressive as *The St. Lawrence and the Saguenay*. When the waste is eliminated, we are left with only a handful of songs and lyrics. Conspicuously, there is no good descriptive poetry in the manuscripts, although it is in his descriptive nature poems in both published volumes that Sangster's poetic gifts are displayed to best advantage. Neither is there any major new piece of work in the manuscripts.

What explanation can be offered for the paucity of good poems in the manuscript collection and the abundance of pieces characterized by the most unfortunate features of Sangster's verse? It would seem that the manuscript poems are the more or less complete literary "remains," rather than a body of work written exclusively, or even primarily, after 1860. "The Rebel," for example, was written in 1839. "Saint Denis," according to a footnote in the manuscripts, was written "many years before Confederation." "With the Iron Duke" belonged, as we noted, to the period of *The St. Lawrence and the Saguenay*. Many others, we may suspect, were written in the 1840's and 1850's and deliberately omitted from the published volumes. Sangster became very excited over his discovery in

W. D. Lighthall of a sympathetic spirit and potential publishing agent. In his initial correspondence with Lighthall he spoke of having had plans to publish a "slim" volume after *Hesperus*, but when it seemed to him that Lighthall might be of assistance he announced that there was too much for one volume and that he was thinking of two. He was an old man by this time—a sick old man tormented by the realization that he had failed to do any important writing or publishing during a period of almost thirty years. Only nineteen of the manuscript poems can definitely be dated after 1860, and most of these are platitudinous occasional verses. Only "Jack, to the Nova Scotians" and two or three of the anthems and martial songs stand out in this group, and it is interesting to notice that even they depend for their effectiveness upon the skills of the rhymer, rather than upon poetic sensibility. There are a few poems in the manuscripts, of course, which do exhibit poetic strength, but there is no reason to suppose that these were written after 1860.

The seeming gap in Sangster's employment between 1861, when he is said to have left the *Whig*, and 1864, when he joined the Kingston *News*, could be of significance. His health may have first broken down about this time. At least we know that by 1868 he was in a low state of health, from which it is to be doubted that he ever fully recovered. The manuscripts demonstrate beyond any reasonable doubt that he lost his poet's gift in the early 1860's and never recovered it.

CHAPTER 7

Summary and Assessment

I Sangster's Ideas

Lorne Pierce correctly observed that Sangster's poetry "exhibits no profound application of ideas to life." All of Sangster's ideas are subservient to his profoundly conventional religious faith. Ultimately, God is the inspiration of his life and poetry. Transcendentalism, rather than pantheism, is his epistemology. His religious faith is infused with pantheism, but it is not dependent upon it. He finds God in nature, but not through nature, because he knows of Him intuitively without the aid of the lessons written in "nature's book." Nature may be "God's church," and the "preacher seas" may nourish his faith, but we get the feeling that at bottom the whole superstructure of nature worship in his poetry is only meant to symbolize real worship in a real church of the real God who lives in heaven. His religious smugness makes him a less patient and intense poet than he might have become had he really been searching for something. He approaches nature for the ostensible purpose of unlocking truths, but since he already knows these truths intuitively, the search is usually cursory at best, and the temptation to wing directly up to God is almost always irresistible. And since his pantheism is only a servant of a priori knowledge, he does not trouble his head over the metaphysical problems created by superimposing one concept of God upon another. If he becomes trapped unwittingly, he simply writes the problem down as another of God's mysteries and as fresh cause for praising his wondrous name. God will enlighten the mind of his blind and bewildered servant after death.

It is quite likely that Sangster would have been incapable of synthesizing his ideas into a coherent philosophy of life even if he had not prostrated himself so dejectedly before a tailor-made one; but "deep thinking," he believes as an article of faith, is the cause of doubt, and doubt is sinful. Whether it was softened by his absolute religious faith or not, his thought is superficial and flabby. Nature is beautiful and inspirational and is the manifestation of God, but the good and evil "spirits of the storm" war with one another; the stars flash hatred at each other across the sky; winter murders by sinister design; and the ocean enfolds its hapless victims with grim delight. How does Sangster reconcile benign nature and malignant nature? He does not, of course, and we suspect that the reason is not only that he cannot find the solution but that he does not care to see the problem. So far as nature's creatures are concerned, he embraces a woozy primitivism. His noble savage, the North American Indian, was without blemish in pre-Columbian times. He was physically, morally, and socially perfect and a stranger, thanks to his healthful environment, to "trouble, sickness, or care." Sangster laments time and again the fact that the Indians were driven from their lands by the Europeans, but the Europeans, it occurs, are just as noble. The mountain dwellers in "Bertram and Lorenzo," Mariline's scholar-shepherd, the husbandman in "A Morning in Summer" with his "noble steed" hauling the "blessed plough," and Sangster's many red-cheeked maidens are quite as perfect as the noble savage in spite of the fact that they now occupy and cultivate his hunting grounds. This is a common enough inconsistency, we may think, but it does not stop there. Just as the Europeans destroyed the way of life of the noble savage, so mechanization and industrialization threaten to destroy the simple way of life of the noble peasant, but, incredibly, Sangster welcomes (at least, at times) the prospect of material progress and "civilization" reaching the villages.[1]

Sangster's cultural primitivism, shallow as it is, is nevertheless consistent with his anti-intellectualism, his snobbery, and his puritanism. Knowledge and wisdom cannot be had from books alone, he believes, because nature is the only true teacher. Thinking and study undertaken in an "unnatural" setting produce pedantry and skepticism, if not a monstrous atheism. Like intellectuality, wealth and rank should be scorned. The highborn (with the notable exception of royalty and military heroes) are vain, heartless, and miserable. But even more contemptible than the educated, the moneyed, or the titled are those who corrupt their bodies with alcohol. Pedants are doomed to sneering their lives away in chilly halls of learning, the privileged to pining theirs away in the boredom of their boudoirs; but all who partake of the forbidden beverage are condemned to a swift and wretched passing from the surface of the earth. These frayed threads of Wordsworthian idealism, Burnsian proletarianism, Calvinistic self-righteousness, and temperance-society tub-thumping are the warp and woof of his social philosophy.

Sangster's ambivalence on the subject of love results from his failure to reconcile religious idealism and Victorian prudishness with emotional reality. Passion, which he condemns as sinful, with puritanical sternness— and yet, we sense, with a tinge of regret—could scarcely be expected to keep easy company with a theory of love as grand (save from the grammatical standpoint) as the one enunciated in the following lines from "Margery":

> Man has but one great love—his love of God;
> All other loves are lesser and more less
> As they recede from Him, as are the streams
> The farthest from the fountain. . . .

"Sangster's guard is almost always up," says E. K. Brown, in speaking of the poet's reluctance or incapacity to express strong emotion. Sangster's love poems tell us as much about the puritanism and squeamishness of his readers as they do of any inadequacy on his part to deal with the subject realistically. Difficult as it is to believe today, his prim pieces were actually considered by his Canadian contemporaries to be brazen. "Mr. Chauveau (Superintendent of Education in Quebec)," said Sangster, in one of his letters, "wrote me that there was too much love in both my volumes to use them for school purposes. Not so bad for a Frenchman—but I fear he was right."[2] And writing as late as 1906, Archibald MacMurchy said that Sangster's "grand theme was love—the noblest of themes; yet it is an open question whether he would not be more acceptable to the general public had he restrained his inclination in this direction."[3] No doubt Sangster feared his reading public as much as he feared the "human Niagara" of passion itself.

On the subject of Canadian nationalism, Sangster's voice is unfaltering, and his vision of a new Canada may be as close as he ever came to an unclouded idea. His dream is of a free "nation" within the British Empire, reaching from the Atlantic to the Pacific. It is not a loose federation of semi-independent states or provinces of which he speaks; it is a fully unified nation ("One voice, one people. . . .") on the British plan, speaking the English language from coast to coast:

> One with her, the mighty Mother,
>   Britain, from whose loins we sprung;
> True to her, to one another,
>   Proud of her beloved tongue.[4]

National unity was regarded as the highest good in Sangster's home province of Canada West in the 1850's and 1860's because of frustration over the fact that the legislature of the Canadian union was split down the center on the basis of language and religion—English and Protestant versus French and Catholic.

[137]

T. G. Marquis says that in his patriotic poems such as "Brock," "Wolfe," and "A Song for Canada," Sangster "did much to foster the national sentiment that seven years later culminated in Confederation." W. H. Robb says that "Sangster's poetry did much to build a national feeling of unity in the people." "Indeed," continues Robb, "some opinion, I found, claims that Confederation was the joint work of Sangster and Macdonald." These are wild claims. National "sentiment," to the extent that it developed at all, was confined almost entirely to Ontario at the time of Confederation, and indeed most of it has remained there. Confederation was not a culmination of sentiment but the most practical means of interring the hopelessly deadlocked parliament of the old Canada. With New Brunswick and Nova Scotia included in the new Canada, there would be a clear English-speaking, Protestant majority in the central legislature. Secondarily, it was recognized that union was vital to defense against possible American invasion. Because of Great Britain's equivocal stand on the Civil War and various border incidents, there was vocal sentiment in the northern states in the mid-1860's in favor of annexation of Canada by force of arms. R. P. Baker puts the case for Sangster's influence more modestly. "It is Sangster's distinction," says Baker, "that he felt the pulse of the national spirit which was beginning to beat, however faintly, throughout Ontario." The truth about the political significance of Sangster's poetry probably lies somewhere between the inference that he helped to quicken the nationalistic pulse in his native Ontario and the heretical opinion of J. E. Collins, a biographer of Sir. John A. Macdonald, and a contemporary of both Macdonald and Sangster. Far from regarding Sangster's verse as contributing in any way to Canadian nationalism, Collins thought, and had the un-Canadian candor to say that it was "not worth a brass farthing."[5]

"So thin is the vein he worked," says T. G. Marquis, "that during the last thirty years of his life he wrote but very little poetry." There are other reasons why Sangster wrote so little during his later years, but in delving for his fundamental ideas, we cannot but be struck by the thinness of the vein of thought, at any rate, from which he mined his lines. After we have tentatively excused him for not being a philosopher, for having none but the most complacent of social attitudes, and for being unable to write convincingly of love (and having given him credit for being on the side of the angels, at least, in his nationalist viewpoint), the barrenness of his mind is still disturbing. There is something Pavlovian about the nature of his responses. For example, he admired to regard the sky as the paradigm of the human visage; the eyes are stars, frowns are clouds, the brain is the guiding intelligence and mysterious deep from which the stars peep forth.

This is the stuff of imagery, but he becomes conditioned by his own conceit to the point that he cannot respond to eyes, for instance, except as stars—"And looking on those orbs of light, I see/ Two guiding stars...." We can be almost certain too that when he thinks eyes he thinks not only stars, but brown, dark, and soft as well. Similarly, when he thinks Indians he thinks no records—of the origin of the Indians. When he thinks dawn or evening he thinks morning or evening star. When he thinks suffering he thinks learning from it. When he thinks mystery he thinks man's limited mind. When he thinks drunkard he thinks long-suffering drunkard's wife. The list could be extended. Marquis would not have known, in all likelihood, of the illness to which Sangster was prone in his later years, but his point is suggestive nonetheless. What else, indeed, had Sangster to say? Sangster leaves us with a thought (one that he expressed only once) which helps ever so slightly to still the urge to tear him for his bad verses. Lorenzo says to Bertram: "In searching for the one great Truth, beware/ Lest thou reject the lesser truths which heaven/Profusely scatters in thy daily path."

II *Sangster as a "Canadian" Poet*

If Sangster does not stand out because of the originality or soundness of his ideas, does he have a Canadian distinctiveness which entitles him to a place in a class apart from other nineteenth-century poets who wrote in English? Sangster's contemporary critics, notably H. J. Morgan and E. H. Dewart, thought so. In his introduction of "Mr. Charles Sangster, the Poet," in his *Sketches of Celebrated Canadians* (1862), Morgan said: "We in Canada are unfortunate enough not to have had many persons entitled to the distinction of being marked as poets, though possessing every facility that a grand and romantic scenic country presents, capable of exiting the proper inspiration and spirit of poetry.... The gentleman whose name heads this notice stands in the first rank of our Canadian poets." This is what many of the reviewers said when Sangster's books were published a few years previously: at long last, here is a distinctively Canadian voice. E. H. Dewart is both more thorough and more splendid on the point in the introduction to his *Selections From Canadian Poets* (1864):

We are disposed to think that any just estimate of Mr. Sangster's poetry will assign him the first place among Canadian poets. Others may have written as well and as sweetly on some themes as he could have done; but no one has contributed so largely to enrich Canadian poetry. No one has attempted so much. No one has displayed equal freshness and variety of imagery in the treatment of national themes. Indeed, in the variety of subjects selected from the scenery, seasons and past history of this country, and in the success and originality with which he has treated them, he has no competitor whatever. His genius is more truly Canadian than that of any other poet of distinction in this Province. Mr. Sangster, while cherishing a loyal attachment to the mother-land, gives Canada the chief place in his heart. Her mighty lakes and rivers—her forests and hills—her history, religion and laws—her homes and liberties—her brave sons and fair daughters—are all objects of his most ardent affection, graven alike upon the pages of his poetry and upon the tablets of his heart.

Writing in 1898, after Roberts, Carman, Lampman, and D. C. Scott had established their reputations, Dewart defended his earlier assessment of Sangster. "In some important respects," Dewart said, "Sangster is still the most representative of our Canadian bards. It is not merely that his themes are Canadian; he lived in an atmosphere of Canadian sentiment, and everything he wrote is permeated with the free spirit of the 'grand old woods' and broad lakes of his country."

Other early commentators on Sangster tended to echo Dewart's opinion, but Dewart and Morgan and their followers were deluding themselves. In fact, it was probably they who seduced Sangster into fancying himself a distinctively Canadian poet, with a peculiarly Canadian mission. His commission to write "Brock" in 1859 may have helped too, but fed by commentary such as Dewart's it is not surprising that he came to regard himself as Canada's poet laureate. That he did so is quite apparent from the large number of occasional verses and Canadian songs in the manuscripts, as well as from statements to be found in his letters to W. D. Lighthall. While Sangster's patriotic verse leaves no doubt about his Canadianism, it does not alter the character of the bulk of his work. At the risk of splitting hairs, it can be said that Sangster was both a Canadian who wrote patriotic verse and a poet who lived in Canada, but that he was not basically a "Canadian" poet. His best poetry is not Canadian at all but English both in spirit and content. Mariline and her scholar-shepherd, the happy harvesters, and the shepherd and the milkmaid in "Lost and Found" would probably have felt as much at home in Tibet as in Canada. In spite of Sangster's best efforts, in many of his nature poems in particular, to think Canadian, his imitative diction evokes a world so unmistakably English that, though he were to mention all of the Indians and maple trees in Canada, he could not dislodge the impression. The following couplet from "Gertrude" is one of the tidiest miniatures he has left us of his Canada: "Underneath the maple trees/Zephyrs chant her melodies."

Sangster is an unwilling Bertram, closeted with his books, rather than a Lorenzo, motivated by the natural world around him. He holds the mirror up, not to nature, but to the works of other poets, who are re-creating a world which lies beyond the shores and borders of Canada. Why should Sangster, who wanted to be a "Canadian" poet, have failed to find a distinctively Canadian voice? E. H. Dewart provided the answer to this question in the introduction to his *Selections*. "Our colonial position," wrote Dewart, "whatever may be its political advantages, is not favorable to the growth of an indigenous literature. Not only are our mental wants supplied by the brain of the Mother Country, under circumstances that utterly preclude competition; but the majority of persons of taste and education in Canada are emigrants from the Old Country, whose tenderest affections cling around the land they have left. The memory of the associations of youth, and of the honored names that have won distinction in every department of human activity, throws a charm around everything that comes from their native land, to which the productions of our young and unromantic country can put forth no claim." By definition, the "colonial mind" does not come to terms with the seemingly harsh, limiting, and uninteresting physical and cultural environment of the colony. E. K. Brown says that a colony "lacks the spiritual energy to rise above routine . . . because it does not adequately believe in itself. It applies to what it has standards which are imported, and therefore artificial and distorting. It sets the great good place not in its present, nor in its past, nor in its future, but somewhere outside its own borders, somewhere beyond its own possibilities."[6] Sangster came closer than any other Canadian poet of his generation to sloughing off the colonial attitude of mind. Had his talents been more prodigious he might have succeeded, but he needed models, and, since there were no Canadian models, he had to look farther afield. He thought to borrow only the forms, through which to channel what he considered to be his uniquely Canadian voice. He did not discover in his lifetime that the medium is also the message.

In preceding chapters we encountered many examples of Sangster's imitativeness. While several commentators have hinted that he was a disciple of one poet or another, none has convincingly demonstrated that this was so. Possibly Wordsworth exerted the most profound single influence on his work, inasmuch as Sangster adopted a modified Wordsworthian nature theory, but his major poem, "The St. Lawrence and the Saguenay," owes more to Byron; and Tennyson's influence is paramount in much of his best work. He is only slightly less indebted to Milton, Burns, Moore, and Longfellow. Although he was a Romantic, his taste was unusually catholic, and he was eclectic in his choice of phrases and images from other poets. A. J. M. Smith mentions one couplet which echoes Pope's *Pastorals*. Here is an equally unlikely echo of a line from John Cleveland:

> And her cheeks—the roses there,
> Like those of York and Lancaster,
> Blended warmly into one,
> Evermore in peace to run.

Shakespeare, Herrick, Herbert, Scott, Coleridge, Shelley, Keats, Poe, Bryant, and even the songwriter Charles Dibdin inspire lines and passages. As we noted earlier, this literary kleptomania is sometimes so obvious that it is insulting, but when the echo is well assimilated, as for example in "Mariline," where Tennyson's "Lady of Shalott" is well in the background, Sangster is sometimes propelled to poetic heights which both surprise and delight.

III *Sangster and His Contemporaries*

In the introduction to his *Canadian Singers and Their Songs* (1919), E. S. Caswell referred to Sangster as the "Father of Canadian Poetry." Throughout the present volume, we have been describing him more modestly as the leading Canadian poet of his generation. What can be said of the nineteenth-century Canadian literary milieu and of Sangster's place in it? "The state of literature, the arts, and sciences in Canada," said John Lambert, an English visitor, in 1810, "can scarcely be said to be at low ebb, because they were never known to flow."[7] This could have been said in 1850 or in 1900 without losing much of its bite. Wilfred Eggleston said it again, in his own way, in 1957 in his book, *The Frontier in Canadian Literature*. Canadian writing before 1900, Eggleston claimed, "consisted of a few collections of poetry, three or four historical works, a few humorous sketches, [and] an essay or two." Otherwise, nineteenth-century Canadian literature was "crude, derivative, imitative, dull, and stodgy."[8]

The problem was one of quality rather than one of quantity. A surprisingly large number of volumes of both prose and verse were published. Before Sangster brought out his first collection in 1856, literally scores of books of poetry had appeared in Canada—or, rather, in the colonies from which modern Canada was formed—and much verse was featured also in the newspapers and periodicals of the time. Literary activity was especially brisk in the Maritime Provinces, where cultural roots had been transplanted more or less intact by the Loyalists and, to a lesser extent, by educated immigrants from Great Britain. The first Canadian poet to command a measure of international critical attention and to achieve a lasting name, if not a lasting reputation, in Canadian letters was Oliver Goldsmith (1794–1861), a grand-nephew and namesake of the illustrious English poet. Born in Saint Andrews, New Brunswick, the son of a Loyalist, Goldsmith published his three-part book-length poem, *The Rising Village*, in London in 1825 and in Saint John, New Brunswick in 1834. As the title of his poem suggests, the younger Oliver Goldsmith was under the spell of his great-uncle. He employed the heroic couplet to describe the growth of settlement in the Maritimes, but his work is slavishly imitative and quite devoid of poetic insight. Joseph Howe (1804–73), the Benjamin Franklin of Canada, was a somewhat more sensitive and graceful poet than Goldsmith, but he too wrote in an eighteenth-century style, and his busy life left him but little time for his poetry. Not even the names of the other Maritime poets of the first half of the nineteenth century have survived, with the possible exception of John Hunter-Duvar's, whose work is still represented in A. J. M. Smith's *Book of Canadian Poetry*. When pronounced with the names of such figures of the literary dawn as Peter John Allan, Alexander Rae Garvie, Arthur Sladen, Andrew Shiels, Joseph Clinch, Mrs. I. S. Prowse, or Cassie Fairbanks, Charles Sangster's name has the ring of a household word. "The final effect upon the reader of Maritime poetry," writes Fred Cogswell, "is one of impersonality—the dominance of a convention beyond which the poets never ventured. Too many poems might quite as easily have been written by other Maritime poets as by their authors."[9]

The picture was even bleaker in the Canadas. In Lower Canada (later Canada East, and now Quebec), French was the language of the majority, and mercantile activities took precedence over cultural pursuits for most of the English-speaking minority in Montreal. Names such as Levi Adams, Mrs. Anne Cuthbert, or Adam Kidd mean nothing today, and those of Standish O'Grady and William Fitz Hawley mean little more. O'Grady, who was born in Ireland in 1793, settled on a farm near Sorel, where he was cold and unhappy. He employed the heroic couplet in most of his verse, and although his poetry is crude, he is one of the most vigorous and witty of Canada's early versifiers. Hawley (1804–55) published *Quebec, The Harp, and Other Poems* in 1829 and *The Unknown, or Lays of the Forest* in 1831. The titles are deceptive; Hawley wrote about Europe and the Near East, rather than about Canada. He wrote under the spell of Campbell, Moore, and Byron, freely admitting that he was using their poems as models. The most unusual of the early Quebec poets was Charles Heavysege (1816–76), who was introduced briefly in Chapter 2.

Upper Canada (later Canada West, and now Ontario), Sangster's home province, had become the most populous of the provinces by the 1850's, but it did not have a Loyalist aristocracy such as the Maritime Provinces had, nor the cultural stability of these older and smaller colonies. Among early poets were Major John Richardson, Susannah Moodie, and William Kirby—all immigrants and all better known for their prose works. Sangster's only rival at home was Alexander McLachlan (1818—96), whom E. H. Dewart described as "the sweetest and most intensely human of all our Canadian bards."[10] An immigrant from Glasgow, Scotland, McLachlan was one of scores of North American imitators of Robert Burns. He published *Lyrics* (1858), *The Emigrant and Other Poems* (1861), and *Poems and Songs* (1874). A prolific writer of newspaper verse, he was more widely read and popularly admired than Sangster, but quite apart from being imitative, his songs are superficial and not infrequently clumsy and sentimental as well. "The Emigrant," his most ambitious work, is written in dialect; it is tiresome and undistinguished, but it has some lyrical interludes in which we find McLachlan at his best. Sangster was capable of worse lines than the following, for example:

> Soon we entered the woods,
> On the trackless solitudes,
> Where the spruce and cedar made
> An interminable shade;
> And the pine and hemlock stood,
> Monarchs of the solitude,
> And we picked our way along,
> Sometimes right and sometimes wrong;
> For a long and weary day,
> Thus we journeyed on our way,
> Picked a path through swale and swamp,
> And at evening fixed our camp,
> Where a lovely little spring
> Murmured like a living thing.

Though McLachlan at his best is better than Sangster at his worst, even these lines display an amateurishness and poor taste not to be found in Sangster.

As a matter of interest, there were several aspirants to the poet's domain in Sangster's home city of Kingston. Evan MacColl, a Scottish-Canadian, Sangster recognized as a gentlemen, if not as a poet. "You should know Evan MacColl," he wrote, in one of his letters to E. H. Dewart, "and if you ever make any stay in Kingston long enough, make his acquaintance by all means and you will find him every inch a man." But there is a note of contempt rare for Sangster in his mention to Dewart of John Breakenridge: "Do you know anything of our Kingston Breakenridge, Author of *The Crusades and Other Poems*? Since dead—both man and book—but I send you one of the poems with my opinion of the book. . . . He was a lawyer. He hadn't the soul of a poet; and was forever carping at everyone who dared write poetry."

Charles Mair (1838–1927) was not really Sangster's literary contemporary, although he was only sixteen years his junior. Mair's first volume, *Dreamland and Other Poems*, was published in 1868, after Sangster's career had virtually ended. However, the two poets have certain interesting similarities and differences. Both wrote descriptive nature poetry, for example, but Mair was a closer observer of nature than Sangster was. Here are the opening lines of Mair's "August," in which we see him at his best:

> Dull August! Maiden of the sultry days,
> And Summer's latest born! When all the woods
> Grow dim with smoke, and smirch their lively green
> With haze of long-continued drought begot;
> When every field grows yellow, and a plague
> Of thirst dries up its herbage to the root,
> So that the cattle grow quite ribby-lean
> On woody stalks whose juices are all spent;
> Where every fronded fern in mid-wood hid
> Grows sick and yellow with the jaundice heat
> Whilst those on hill-sides glare with patchy red.

Mair is frequently careless, however, and his language is even more consistently conventional than Sangster's. He is also "given to sudden bewildering descents into bathos"[11]—as Desmond Pacey describes it. Here are the lines, from Mair's "Innocence," which Pacey uses to illustrate this point:

> Oft have I seen her walk
> Through flow'r decked fields unto the oaken pass
> Where lay the slumbery flock,
> Swoll'n with much eating of the tender grass.

Mair does not have Sangster's good taste, and few would be so bold as to rank him with Sangster as a poet. On the other hand, none would be so rash as to rank Sangster with Mair as a phenomenon in Canada's literary history. One of the five members of the "Canada First" movement, Mair was an outspoken nationalist and a vigorous activist. Involved in the development of the West, he was taken prisoner and sentenced to death during the first Riel Rebellion in Manitoba. He made a daring escape from his captors, and after many adventures, he gained the Minnesota border and freedom. Mair consciously chose to write on Canadian themes, and his poetry is more distinctly Canadian than Sangster's is. Ever generous in his praise of other Canadian poets (with the exception of Kingston's Breaken-ridge), Sangster spoke as follows of Mair in his letter to William Kirby of April 30, 1886: "Mair sent me a copy of *Tecumseh* through his publishers. It is a worthy following up of his *Dreamland and Other Poems*, and I feel proud of his great success. The book is really very fine and must be a forerunner of far better things to come."

It was not until the 1880's that Sangster's pre-eminence among Canadian poets was challenged, but so swift was the coming of the new order that by 1894, as E. H. Dewart stated, the younger generation of readers were asking: "Who is Charles Sangster? " By this time, Sangster's message had been completely jammed by the faultless notes of Archibald Lampman; the studied dissonance of Duncan Campbell Scott; and the sweet, sad music of Bliss Carman. The harbinger of Canada's first genuine literary movement was Charles G. D. Roberts, who was a twenty-year-old student at the University of New Brunswick in 1880 when his *Orion and Other Poems* was published. The publication of *Orion* was pregnant with significance for Canadian poetry, as Archibald Lampman's response to the appearance of the volume makes clear. "Like most of the young fellows about me," wrote Lampman, "I had been under the depressing conviction that we were hopelessly situated on the outskirts of civilization, where no art and no literature could be, and that it was useless to expect that we could do it ourselves. I sat up most of the night reading and re-reading *Orion* in a state of wildest excitement and when I went to bed I could not sleep. It seemed to me a wonderful thing that such work could be done by a Canadian, by a young man, one of ourselves. It was like a voice from some new paradise of art, calling to us to be up and doing."

Orion marked the beginning of the long, slow death of the colonial attitude of mind in Canadian poetry. The new poets were classically educated young men who took as premise, as Sangster and his contemporaries did not, that the Canadian environment, because it was the only one they knew, would define both the form and the emotion of their art. That they often fell short of realizing their poetic ideals does not much detract from the drama of their advent upon the literary scene. Yet the break with the past was not as clean as it seemed at the time. Like Sangster, the new poets labored within the Romantic tradition, and in a subtler way than he, they too were imitative. Roberts, in particular, began not far from where

Sangster left off, but the relative brilliance of much of the new poetry blinded Canadian literary criticism for many years to all that had preceded it.

Sangster was not the "Father of Canadian Poetry," as E. S. Caswell described him, because he was not an innovator, nor did he have any disciples or imitators. Neither was he a great, or a very good poet. On the other hand, had he been merely a dilettante among lesser dilettantes he would not deserve even a humble place in the literary annals of his country. In spite of the many limiting influences which reach into his work, there is never any doubt that he has a poet's soul and the magic touch of a true artist. His claim upon our memory is a poet's claim, and even though all of his major poems are less than artistically satisfying, his claim is a thoroughly legitimate one. With Sangster and other Canadian poets in mind, Northrop Frye wrote: "Some literary values may emerge from an intense struggle between a poetic imagination and the Canadian environment even if the former is defeated. It is a somewhat narrow view of criticism, and in Canada an impossibly pedantic one, that excludes all sympathy for poets who have tried something big with only a little success."[12]

Notes and References

Chapter One

1. In "Who Was Carl Fechter? " *Historic Kingston*, 12 (1964), 11–18, Professor H. Pearson Gundy develops a case for "Carl Fechter," the author of a series of articles about Kingston and Kingstonians published in the *Daily Whig* in 1886, actually having been Charles Sangster. While they would not add significantly to his literary stature, these first-person articles are more revealing of the personality of their author than are any of Sangster's acknowledged works. "Carl Fechter" displays more urbanity, more humor, more interest in people and politics, and a more idiomatic writing style than we associate with Sangster. Unfortunately, although Professor Gundy's arguments are compelling ones, his evidence is wholly circumstantial. Also, there is serious doubt about Sangster's physical and mental capacity for writing the series. It filled sixteen newspaper pages in all and would have required steady work during the period in which it was running. The first article appeared on October 16, 1886. "I came here in September, 1886," wrote Sangster two years later, "and my native air has made me 50% better, and given me a fair use of my brain, whereas *when I reached here I was not capable of writing the merest note without blundering*." (Letter to Lighthall, November 15, 1888.)

2. Desmond Pacey, "Charles Sangster," in his *Ten Canadian Poets* (Toronto, 1958), p. 1. Unless otherwise noted, references to Professor Pacey's work on Sangster are to this essay: pp. 1–33 in the volume.

3. Public Archives of Canada, Ottawa. The Gibson and Stewart letters are among the David Gibson Papers and the Caron Papers, respectively.

4. A. J. M. Smith, *The Book of Canadian Poetry* (Toronto, 1957; third ed.), p. 100. The incorrect statement is: "He died in Ottawa in 1893." All references to Professor Smith's work on Sangster are to this volume: pp. 7–8, 13–14, 100–101.

5. Quoted in E. H. Dewart, "Charles Sangster, the Canadian Poet," *Canadian Magazine*, VII (May, 1896). Unless otherwise noted, references to Rev. Dr. Dewart's work on Sangster are to this essay: pp. 28–34.

6. Sangster autobiographical fragment in the McGill Collection. Unless otherwise noted, Sangster's words are quoted from this document.

7. The Ross letters are among the Sangster documents in the Douglas Library, Queen's University, Kingston.

8. Lot 13, Con. 2, Hinchinbrooke township, Frontenac county. James Sangster died before issuance of letters patent, and in 1848 John Sangster, tinsmith, of Kingston, claimed the lot as assignee of Hugh Sangster, tinsmith, of Buffalo, New York, eldest son and heir of James Sangster. John's claim was allowed and the lot patented in his name July 25, 1851 (Ontario Department of Public Records and Archives, Toronto).

9. Quoted in J. A. Roy, *Kingston, The King's Town*, (Toronto, 1952), p. 136. Indebtedness to Professor Roy for a number of the factual statements made about nineteenth-century Kingston is hereby acknowledged.

10. *Ibid.*, p. 138.

11. This letter is among the Sangster documents in the Douglas Library, Queen's University, Kingston.

12. This letter is in the McGill Collection.

13. Hugh MacLennan, "Portrait of a City," in *Atlantic Anthology*, ed. by Will R. Bird (Toronto, 1959), p. 285.

14. George Stewart states in "Charles Sangster and His Poetry," *Stewart's Literary Quarterly Magazine*, III (October, 1869), 335, that Sangster was a contributor to *Barker's Canadian Magazine*, which was published at Kingston (1846–47), and several other commentators have repeated the claim. No evidence of this has been found. There was very little poetry published in the magazine, and most of the prose was written by four pseudonymous writers whose identities are not known.

Chapter Two

1. *Chronicle and News* (Kingston, September 19, 1856).

2. All quotations from reviews of *The St. Lawrence and the Saguenay* are as reproduced in an appendix to *Hesperus*.

3. *Daily News* (Kingston, November 3, 1860).

4. See H. Pearson Gundy, "Charles Sangster 1822–1893," *Historic Kingston*, XII (1965), 85.

5. All quotations from reviews of *Hesperus* are as reproduced in Henry J. Morgan's *Sketches of Celebrated Canadians* (Quebec, 1862), pp. 689–91.

6. Bayard Taylor's and Oliver Wendell Holmes's comments are quoted in Henry J. Morgan, *Bibliotheca Canadensis* (Ottawa, 1867), p. 337.

7. *Daily News* (Kingston, April 18, 1863).

8. The volume issued by the Century Club has not been traced, but the facts are stated in Morgan, *Bibliotheca Canadensis*, p. 336, and there is a clipping of the poem in the McGill Collection.

9. Wallace H. Robb, "Charles Sangster, Canada's and Kingston's Poet,"

Historic Kingston, XI (1963). All references to Mr. Robb's work on Sangster are to this article: pp. 30—34.

10. See Pacey, *op. cit.*, p. 15.

11. *Daily News* (Kingston, August 22, 1868).

12. John Reade, "English Literature and Journalism in Quebec," in *Canada: An Encyclopedia of the Country*, vol. 5, p. 155n.

13. See Desmond Pacey, *Creative Writing in Canada* (Toronto, 1952), p. 52.

Chapter Three

1. Following are the street addresses listed for Charles Sangster in Ottawa city directories: 1868—69, Queen; 1870, Stewart; 1871—75, Botelier; October, 1875—78, 281 Maria; 1879—80, 279 Maria; 1882, 556 Maria; 1883—86, 281 Maria; 1892, 412 Lewis.

2. Names and ages for the Sangster family are recorded in the 1871 Canada Census Schedules for Ottawa, District 77, Sub-District C, Saint George's Ward, p. 65 (Public Archives of Canada). In Sangster's letter of April 20, 1886, to William Kirby, he states that his son is seven years of age. The only published reference to the son's name is in E. S. Caswell, *Canadian Singers and their Songs* (Toronto, 1919; rev. ed.), p. 9. "For the photograph," writes Caswell, "the Editor is indebted to Mr. Rod Sangster, of Montreal, a son of the poet."

3. E. K. Brown, *On Canadian Poetry* (Toronto, 1943; rev. ed.). Unless otherwise noted, references to Professor Brown's work on Sangster are to pp. 29—33 of this volume.

4. Gundy, "Charles Sangster 1822—1893," pp. 84—88.

Chapter Four

1. See Isaiah 6, Jeremiah 1, and Amos 7.

2. Quoted in Morgan, *Bibliotheca Canadensis*, p. 336.

3. Stewart, *op. cit.* All references to Mr. Stewart's work on Sangster are to this article: pp. 334—41.

4. W. D. Lighthall, *Songs of the Great Dominion* (London, 1889), p. xxv. Unless otherwise noted, references to Dr. Lighthall's work on Sangster are to this volume: pp. xxv—xxvi.

5. R. P. Baker, "Charles Sangster," in his *History of English-Canadian Literature to the Confederation* (Cambridge, Mass., 1920). All references to Professor Baker's work on Sangster are to this chapter: pp. 159—65.

6. J. D. Logan and D. G. French, *Highways of Canadian Literature* (Toronto, 1924). All references to the work of Professors Logan and French on Sangster are to this volume: pp. 97—99.

7. Lorne Pierce, *Outline of Canadian Literature* (Toronto, 1927). All

references to Dr. Pierce's work on Sangster are to this volume: pp. 65–66.

8. Arthur S. Bourinot, "Charles Sangster (1822–1893)," *Educational Record* (Quebec), LXII (July–September, 1946). All references to Mr. Bourinot's work on Sangster are to this article: pp. 179–85.

9. Louis Dudek, "Literature in English," in *The Canadians*, ed. by J. M. S. Careless and R. C. Brown (Toronto, 1967). pp. 643–44.

10. Letter to Lighthall (July 14, 1891).

11. Letter to Lighthall (September 9, 1891).

12. Morgan, *Bibliotheca Canadensis*, p. 335.

13. Letter to Lighthall (July 18, 1888).

Chapter Five

1. Anon., "Charles Sangster," in *A Cyclopedia of Canadian Biography* (Toronto, 1888), p. 423.

2. T. G. Marquis, "English Canadian Literature," in *Canada and Its Provinces*, ed. by Adam Shortt (Toronto, 1914), vol. 12. All references to Professor Marquis' work on Sangster are to this volume: pp. 568–69.

3. Gundy, "Charles Sangster 1822–1893," p. 87.

Chapter Six

1. Amos W. Sangster was a son of the poet's brother Hugh. See note 8 under Chapter 1.

2. See C. C. James, *Bibliography of Canadian Poetry* (Toronto, 1899), p. 57.

3. Sangster provides information of this sort in notes in the manuscripts.

4. Morgan, *Sketches of Celebrated Canadians*, p. 688.

5. *Saturday Reader*, I (January 13, 1866), 297.

6. Genealogy Department, Buffalo and Erie County Public Library, provided this information.

Chapter Seven

1. Donald B. Gammon's unpublished thesis, "The Concept of Nature in Nineteenth Century Canadian Poetry" (University of New Brunswick, 1948), was helpful in the study of Sangster's nature theory.

2. Quoted in Dewart, *op. cit.*, p. 31.

3. Archibald MacMurchy, *Handbook of Canadian Literature* (Toronto, 1906), p. 73.

4. From "July First 1867."

5. Quoted in *A Cyclopedia of Canadian Biography*, p. 424.

6. Brown, *op. cit.*, p. 14.

7. Quoted in H. Pearson Gundy, "Literary Publishing," in *Literary History of Canada* (Toronto, 1965), p. 175.

8. *Ibid.*, p. 174.

9. Fred Cogswell, "Literary Activity in the Maritime Provinces 1815–1880," in *Literary History of Canada*, p. 105.

10. E. H. Dewart, *Selections From Canadian Poets* (Montreal, 1864), p. xxvii.

11. Pacey, *Creative Writing in Canada*, p. 35.

12. Northrop Frye, "Poetry," in *The Arts in Canada*, ed. by Malcolm Ross (Toronto, 1958), p. 85.

Selected Bibliography

PRIMARY SOURCES

The St. Lawrence and the Saguenay and Other Poems. Auburn, New York: Miller, Orton, and Mulligan, 1856.
Hesperus and Other Poems and Lyrics. Montreal: John Lovell, 1860.
Our Norland. Toronto: Copp, Clarke Company, n.d.

SECONDARY SOURCES

ANON. "Charles Sangster," in *A Cyclopedia of Canadian Biography*. Toronto: Rose Publishing Company, 1888, pp. 423–24.

BAKER, R. P. "Charles Sangster," in his *A History of English-Canadian Literature to the Confederation*. Cambridge: Harvard University Press, 1920, pp. 159–65. One of the most scholarly treatments of Sangster's work. Baker regards Sangster to be the Longfellow of Canada.

BOURINOT, ARTHUR S. "Charles Sangster (1822–1893)," *Educational Record* (Quebec), 62 (July–September, 1946), pp. 179–85. [Also in *Leading Canadian Poets*, ed. by W. P. Percival. Toronto: Ryerson Press, 1948, pp. 202–12. Also in his *Five Canadian Poets*. Montreal: Quality Press, 1956, pp. 8–14.] The most significant biographical article to appear between 1896 and 1958–largely superseded by Pacey's work, but still of interest.

BROWN, E. K. "The Problem of a Canadian Literature," and "The Development of Poetry in Canada," in his *On Canadian Poetry*, rev. ed. Toronto: Ryerson Press, 1943, pp. 1–87. Though only pp. 29–33 are devoted to Sangster, this penetrating and lucid critique of Canadian poetry and culture is a valuable aid to perspective.

DEWART, E. H. "Introductory Essay," in his *Selections From Canadian Poets*. Montreal: Lovell, 1864, pp. ix–xix. The first important essay on Canadian poetry and the chief critical boost given Sangster's poetry during his lifetime.

——. "Charles Sangster, the Canadian Poet," *Canadian Magazine*, VII (May, 1896), 29–34. The principal nineteenth-century essay on Sangster. It is still of biographical interest, because Dewart quotes letters received from Sangster and includes two photographs of the poet.

——. "Charles Sangster, a Canadian Poet of the Last Generation," in his *Essays For the Times*. Toronto: Briggs, 1898, pp. 38–51. The same essay which was published in the *Canadian Magazine*, with the photographs omitted and one brief paragraph added.

GAMMON, DONALD B. "The Concept of Nature in Nineteenth Century Canadian Poetry, with Special Reference to Goldsmith, Sangster, and Roberts" (Thesis, University of New Brunswick, 1948).

GUNDY, H. PEARSON. "Who Was Carl Fechter? " *Historic Kingston*, 12 (1964), 11–18.

——. "Charles Sangster 1822–1893," *Historic Kingston*, 13 (1965), 84–88.

HAMILTON, W. D. "An Edition of the Hitherto Uncollected Poems of Charles Sangster, together with a Biographical and Critical Introduction and Notes" (Thesis, University of New Brunswick, 1958).

LIGHTHALL, W. D. "Introduction," in his *Songs of the Great Dominion*. London: Scott, 1889, pp. xxv–xxvi. There is also a short biographical sketch on p. 461.

LOGAN, J. D. and FRENCH, D. G. *Highways of Canadian Literature*. Toronto: McClelland and Stewart, 1924, pp. 97–99. Interesting only for its emphasis on Sangster's Canadianism.

MACMURCHY, ARCHIBALD. *Handbook of Canadian Literature*. Toronto: Briggs, 1906, pp. 71–75.

MARQUIS, T. G. "English-Canadian Literature," in *Canada and Its Provinces*, ed. by Adam Shortt. Toronto: Glasgow Brook, 1914, vol. 12, pp. 568–69.

MORGAN, HENRY J. "Mr. Charles Sangster, the Poet," in his *Sketches of Celebrated Canadians*. Quebec: Hunter Rose, 1862, pp. 684–93. Of value chiefly for the reviews of *Hesperus* from which Morgan quotes.

——. "Charles Sangster," in his *Bibliotheca Canadensis*. Ottawa: Desbarats, 1867, pp. 335–37.

PACEY, DESMOND. "Charles Sangster," in his *Ten Canadian Poets*. Toronto: Ryerson Press, 1958, pp. 1–33. Contains by far the most informative biography of Sangster and the most comprehensive review of his poetry.

PIERCE, LORNE. *An Outline of Canadian Literature*. Toronto: Ryerson Press, 1927, pp. 65–66.

RHODENIZER, V. B. *A Handbook of Canadian Literature.* Ottawa: Graphic, 1930, pp. 164–65.

ROBB, WALLACE HAVELOCK. "Charles Sangster, Canada's and Kingston's Poet," *Historic Kingston*, 11 (1963), 30–34.

SMITH, A. J. M. "Introduction," in his *The Book of Canadian Poetry*, third ed. Toronto: Gage, 1957, pp. 7–8, 13–14. There are also biographical and critical notes on pp. 100–101 of this volume. This is the standard contemporary anthology of Canadian poetry, and Sangster's work is better represented in this volume than in any other. Also, Professor Smith's critical remarks are eminently sound.

STEWART, GEORGE. "Charles Sangster and His Poetry," *Stewart's Literary Quarterly Magazine*, 3 (October, 1869), 334–41.

BACKGROUND SOURCES

ROY, J. A. *Kingston, The King's Town.* Toronto: McClelland and Stewart, 1952.

WAY, RONALD L. "Old Fort Henry, the Citadel of Upper Canada," *Canadian Geographical Journal*, 40 (April, 1950), 149–69.

Index

Index

Index